N

Trentino-
Alto Adige
13
12
8
3   5
Lombardia   Veneto   9
10
11
Friuli-
Venezia
Giulia

16   15
Emilia-
Romagna   14

ria

17
Toscana

Marche
18   19
Umbria

21   Abruzzi
Lazio   22
20   Molise   25
24   24   27
35   Puglia
Campania   24
32   31   30   34   28   26
33   Basilicata   37   29
36

Calabria
39
40

38

Sardegna
47

50

42   43
46   Sicilia
44   41
45

Father Orsini's Pasta Perfetta

Father Orsini's
Pasta Perfetta

Father Joseph Orsini

Hearst Books / New York

Library of Congress Cataloging-in-Publication Data

Orsini, Joseph E.
    Father Orsini's pasta perfetta / by Joseph Orsini.
      p.   cm.
    Includes index.
    ISBN 0-688-13520-X
    1. Cookery (Pasta) 2. Cookery, Italian. I. Title.
TX809.M17077 1995
641.8'22—dc20   94-22326
                                          CIP

Printed in the United States of America

First Edition

1 2 3 4 5 6 7 8 9 10

BOOK DESIGN BY RICHARD ORIOLO
ENDPAPER MAP AND ILLUSTRATION BY KRIS TOBIASSEN

To my beloved brother Oreste,
who made my life joyful.
He died December 12, 1992, but lives
on in the happy memories
he left behind.

Foreword by Jeff Smith,
The Frugal Gourmet

The word *orsini* in Italian means "little bear." The fact that children in Father Orsini's parish refer to him as Papa Bear should give you some clue as to the warmth of character that you are going to find in this book.

The guy is a kick—a child of the Church, surely, and also a joy. I know that this confuses some people since they figure that the clergy should quietly eat bad food and put up with a boring life-style. Not so with Father Orsini!

Brother priests adore this man because he will cook for them. His family loves his presence because he believes the table is the proper place for real celebration. He sees a profound connection between the family dinner table and the altar of the Church. He shares bread and wine with us in two ways—on behalf of the family and on behalf of the Creator.

Further, he claims that God is actually Italian and loves pasta. Therefore, this culinary catechism.

Don't bother to look for complicated and fancy recipes here. They are basic, down-to-earth food for the people. You will find dishes that will become favorites, and you will be proud of yourself since you can cook almost of them in a hurry.

Read the last recipe in the book, now, a dish called Addictive Pasta. You will understand what I mean. I love this man and I love his pasta.

Acknowledgments

I wish to thank the following family members and friends:

Leo and Inez Orsini

John and Marie Orsini

Dominick and Mary Orsini

Anthony and Marie Orsini

Joseph and Evelyn Varela

Carmel and Judge Carmen Ferrante

Carmel and Glenn Cricco

Ann and Sandy Davidson

Mary E. Orsini

Leo and Caroline Orsini

Joseph and Janet Orsini

Catherine Orsini Peacock

Denise Orsini Berkery and Thomas Berkery

Joseph and Gertrude Orsini

Francisco and Debbie Varela

Oreste and Karen Varela

Kenneth and Trinidad Walter

Inez C. Orsini

Jo-Anne Orsini Martin

Anna and Reggie Conti

Santa Fiorivanti

Richard Conti

Helen Barberio

Caroline and Bill Napoli

Frank and Elsie Napoli

Rachel Napoli Budd

Harry Dombrosky

Clifford Barr

The Benanti Family

Charles and Oksana Pestritto

Anthony and Felicia Repice

Dr. Sal and Rosemarie Cerniglia

The Di Mauro Family

Vincenzo Calderone

D. Anthony Pullella

The Gaglioti Family

The Sestito Family, Nicholas and Dee

Joseph and Valerie Cassano

Nick and Rita Giordano

Anthony Oswald

Cuono Chiricolo

Daniel E. Hughes

Salvatore Vassallo

Contents

Introduction

When my second Italian cookbook, *Father Orsini's Italian Kitchen* (St. Martin's Press, 1991), was published, my publicist, John Murphy, dubbed me the Pope of Pasta—the Cardinal of Cuisine. At first I was rather embarrassed by these nicknames, but after some time I became accustomed to them.

The publicity that attended my book, especially my appearances on television, convinced me that I must continue to write. The idea for this volume came to me while studying the geography and history of Italy.

Italy is composed of twenty geographical regions and each region has its own particular history, language, and cuisine. With this book you will be able to visit each region and taste the pasta specialties of the whole Italian peninsula and its islands without the expense of air travel and lodging. I've focused on pasta recipes because to include all of the gastronomy of Italy would require an encyclopedia.

The country that is famous for its indescribable works of art has summoned me to its delightful shores thirty-four times since 1959. Like the sirens of classical legend, whose mesmerizing songs led hapless sailors to their destruction, Italy has summoned me with its siren song. The only destruction I suffered was temporary, however, when I gained a few pounds from the magnificent meals I enjoyed, but which I quickly lost after doing what the Italians do—walk, walk, walk, and diet, diet, diet.

In October 1992 and again in 1993 I willingly and happily returned to the land of sun, song, and pasta, where I discovered that the making and eating of pasta is indeed a seriously fine art. It is perhaps not as esteemed as painting, architecture, sculpture, or music, but just as important in the evolving history of the human experience. For pasta is often the dramatic and satisfying first act in the fine art of cementing the strong bonds that characterize the Italian family.

My first research journey brought me to Reggio Calabria, my parents' birthplace. While there I stayed at the Archbishop's residence because I wanted to be in a place where I could celebrate daily Mass. I especially enjoyed the company of Monsignor Giuseppe Caruso, who is a wonderfully gracious and kind man. I consider it an honor to call him both friend and colleague.

Monsignor Caruso and I were able to spend some time together to deepen our friendship. It was through him that I discovered that the church in Reggio Calabria was founded by St. Paul. Researching the history of the archdiocese, I discovered, much to my delight, that there had been in its long history two bishops named Orsini.

On a much earlier trip to Italy, I was the guest at the magnificent dining room table of Ermenegildo Florit, the Cardinal Archbishop of Florence. After leading us in a prayer of thanks to God for what we were about to enjoy and share, this wonderful man of God looked at me and said, "*Caro Don Giuseppe, la pasta è la poesia della tavola, la mangiaremo con rispetto e con gusto, perche è veramente un arte come tutte le altre belle arti.*" "Dear Father Joseph, *pasta is the poetry of the table,* we will eat it with respect and delight because it is indeed an art like all the other fine arts."

Come with me, dear reader, and discover the marvelous world of Italian pasta.

A Note to Readers

Because I want you to share my enjoyment of the Italian table, I've arranged the recipes geographically in three sections—Northern Italy, Central Italy, and Southern Italy. Within each section I usually indicate what region a particular dish comes from and tell you the name of the city, town, or village where I first tasted it.

In the course of enjoying the food that you cook, you will no doubt want to enhance your pleasure with appropriate wines from a particular area. And if you're planning a trip to Italy, you will surely want to dine at restaurants that feature local fare. Therefore, I've included information on wines and restaurants following the recipes of each section. (Please note that in some cases a wine will carry the designation DOC, indicating that it is a product of a particular region—see page 35 for a full explanation.)

Including these extras in the book enables you to accompany me on my travels from northern Italy to the southernmost spot of this diverse and delightful country.

Father Joseph Orsini

Father Orsini's Pasta Perfetta

A Few Basics

1. **Black Pepper:** It is always better to buy peppercorns and grind your own. The pepper will be fresher, more aromatic, and less expensive.

2. **Tomato Sauce:** Of course, it is always better to make your own, see page 3 but canned tomato sauce can be used in an emergency.

3. **Grated Cheese:** Pecorino Romano is more robust than Parmesan, which is finer and more delicate. The taste of these cheeses is more genuine when bought by the piece and grated as needed.

4. **Wines and Liquors:** When cooked, these beverages lose their alcohol through evaporation. All that remains is the flavor, so they may be used even by those who wish to avoid alcohol.

5. **Soup Stocks:** Of course, stocks are better when one makes them fresh, but a perfectly suitable substitution is canned stock or bouillon cubes dissolved in water.

6. **Tomatoes:** I recommend canned Italian peeled plum tomatoes. To sweeten tomato sauce, one tablespoon of sugar will do. If you wish to avoid sugar, wash, peel, and dice finely a large carrot and sauté in the saucepan for ten minutes over low heat before adding other ingredients.

7. **Pasta:** Generally speaking, if the pasta that a particular recipe calls for is unavailable, use spaghetti when long pasta (such as fettuccine) is indicated, rigatoni for macaroni (or other tube shapes).

8. **Dairy Products:** If you are trying to cut fat from your diet or lower your cholesterol, you may use low or nonfat substitutes in place of whole dairy products. For example, use low-fat creamy cottage cheese in place of

ricotta. Instead of butter, use low-fat margarine. Instead of whole milk, use skim milk. Instead of whole-milk mozzarella, use part-skim mozzarella.

9. **Salt:** Salt may be eliminated completely from any recipe, although it will affect its flavor. I use regular salt.

10. **Dried Mushrooms:** These must always be rehydrated in lukewarm water, then drained through cheesecloth or the finest wire mesh possible to remove grit. The sand and dirt will remain behind and the mushroom liquid may be used to enrich sauces and stocks.

11. **Oil:** Olive oil is recommended because of its exquisite flavor and the complete absence of cholesterol. However, any good vegetable oil may be substituted.

12. **Cooking Pasta:** Use a large pasta pot and abundant water. Bring the water to a rolling boil, add the pasta, and stir constantly so that the pasta will not stick together. You may also add a tablespoon of oil and salt, if you wish, after the pasta has been added and the water has returned to a boil.

13. **Herbs:** Wherever possible, use fresh herbs. The dried varieties must be used sparingly—only one teaspoon unless otherwise indicated.

14. **Eggplant:** Unless otherwise indicated, always follow this procedure when preparing eggplant: Slice the eggplant, layer it in a colander, and sprinkle liberally with salt. Allow it to degorge itself of bitter liquid for at least one half hour, wash the slices, pat dry, and then follow cooking instructions.

15. **Julienne:** This technique involves cutting vegetables or meat into slivers the size of kitchen matchsticks.

Basic Tomato Sauce

2 2-pound 3-ounce cans Italian plum tomatoes

2 large onions, peeled and diced

5 large garlic cloves, peeled and diced

¼ cup olive oil

½ tablespoon salt

1 teaspoon freshly ground black pepper

1 teaspoon oregano

16 leaves fresh basil, washed and torn, or 1 teaspoon dry basil

1 tablespoon sugar

Chop the tomatoes in a blender for 1 minute until pureed and set aside.

In a large saucepan sauté onion and garlic in olive oil until onion is lightly browned. Add tomatoes and remaining ingredients. Stir and bring to a boil. Lower heat and simmer covered for 2 hours, stirring occasionally.

This sauce freezes well and may be used in any recipe that calls for tomato sauce. This can be made into a meat sauce simply by adding 1 pound of lean ground beef to the pan after sautéing the onion and garlic. Brown meat well and continue recipe.

Makes 10 cups

Bechamel Sauce

4 tablespoons butter

¼ cup all-purpose flour

2½ cups boiling hot milk

Salt and pepper to taste

Dash of nutmeg

In a small saucepan, melt butter over low heat. Add flour, stir with wooden spoon, and cook for several minutes without browning the roux. Remove from heat, and stir in the hot milk gradually, mixing until smooth.

Return to heat and stir until boiling, then simmer for ten minutes. Season with salt and pepper to taste. Stir in a dash of nutmeg. This sauce will stay fresh in refrigerator for at least 3 days. However, I recommend making it fresh each time a recipe calls for bechamel.

Makes 2 cups

Homemade Pasta

4 eggs

2½ to 3 cups all-purpose flour

I use a standing electric mixer to make this pasta. Of course, it can be done by hand, but it takes much longer and is a tiresome exercise.

Beat eggs until frothy. Add flour a little at a time until doughy. Change to dough hook, and knead for 5 minutes. Place dough in unfloured container, cover with plastic wrap, and let rest in refrigerator for ½ hour.

Take half the dough, knead it lightly, and shape it into a ball. Place on well-floured surface, flatten dough, and sprinkle with flour. Roll out dough with rolling pin, sprinkling with flour as necessary so that dough does not stick to rolling pin. Roll dough, trying to keep it in a round disk, as thin as possible. Do the same with the other half of the dough. Use as directed in each individual recipe.

Chapter 1

The Hearty Fare
of
Northern Italy

Introducing the Region

Before the unification of the Italian peninsula and its islands by Giuseppe Garibaldi in 1860, Italy was simply a geographical location. Its land and its peoples belonged to other nations, kings, or city-states controlled by powerful families. (Even today, there are two independent countries within Italy's borders: the Republic of San Marino and Vatican City.)

By 1870, however, Italy had begun to emerge as a unified modern nation, and the Tuscan dialect was selected as the national language.

Yet, despite unification, each region, each locality, each town, city, and village has retained its own proper history and even its own dialect.

It follows, then, that there is no such thing as one Italian cuisine. Rather there are many regional Italian cuisines, multifaceted and with many distinctive styles, each one bespeaking the traditions of its region.

We begin our journey in the *Valle d'Aosta* on the French border. The language of the region is, for all practical purposes, French, creating a bilingual population that speaks its own French dialect as well as Italian.

Neighboring Valle d'Aosta is *Piemonte*, which means "at the feet of the mountains," referring to nature's towers, the Alps. The language, again, is a French dialect and, of course, everyone reads, writes, and speaks Italian.

Lombardia borders the Italian-speaking canton of Switzerland. Its capital is Milan, the New York City of Italy. Milan is the richest commercial center of the country, setting the latest fashion trends for all of Europe, and offering some of the finest northern Italian fare in its many restaurants.

A short distance from Milan is the lake region, studded with gemlike towns and villages. My favorite town is Stresa, on the edge of Lago Maggiore. I always try to end my trips to Italy by spending a few days in Stresa, to wind down before returning to the frenetic United States.

Domodossola, an Italian-Swiss village near the border in the Alps, is typically alpine and reminds one of the movie *Heidi*. It was here that the *bersaglieri*, crack troops of Italian sharpshooters, defended the borders of Italy from foreign invaders.

Within Lombardia is Mantova, a medieval town, where in earlier times the famous Roman poet Vergil wrote the *Aeneid*, the Latin version of the Greek epics the *Iliad* and the *Odyssey*. The hero of the *Aeneid* is the Trojan Aeneas who escapes the destruction of Troy and eventually finds his way to the river Tiber, where he establishes the city of Rome.

In *Liguria* there is an appropriately named town, Ventimiglia, which means "twenty miles," its distance from the Provence region of France. This whole area was once the domain of the king of Savoy, Victor Emmanuel II, who became the first king of Italy in 1870.

Liguria is the home of the port of Genoa, the birthplace of Christopher Columbus, and thus plays a unique role in the European discovery of America. It is a geographically small region, but its role in Italian history is im-

mense. The cuisine of Liguria is refreshing and richly satisfying.

Veneto comprises what was once the independent and powerful Republic of Venice. Although it is now adjacent to a heavily industrialized area, Venice, the serene city of canals built on a lagoon, still draws thousands of visitors every year. Indeed, it is called La Serenissima by the Venetians.

Padova (which can be reached from Venice by canal as well as by car) is the site of the ascetic church of St. Anthony of Padua. A Franciscan monk, Saint Anthony was a famous preacher. When his body was exhumed during the process of his canonization (the official recognition of sainthood by the Catholic Church), there was nothing left of the body except the tongue. This did not decay, and can now be viewed by his devotees in the church.

Friuli-Venezia Giulia borders the former Yugoslavia. In fact, the whole Adriatic coastline of the former Yugoslavia was once Italian territory. There, Slavic Croatians are bilingual, speaking Slavic Croatian and Italian as do the Italians of the region. Often the cuisine of Friuli-Venezia Giulia is an Italian adaptation of Slavic fare.

Trentino-Alto Adige, an extremely mountainous region, has two important cities, Trento and Bolzano. This region borders Austria, and although the population is Italian, Germanic influence predominates: in custom (little wine is consumed here; beer reigns supreme); in language (the everyday language is German; Italian is spoken only when necessary); and in cuisine (sauerkraut, Wiener Schnitzel, and strudel are everyday fare). The street signs are written in both German and Italian.

Emilia-Romagna is the location of Bologna, where many of the streets boast colonnades, and tourists can visit the oldest university in the Western world. Its cuisine is so rich that it is called Bologna, La Grassa, or "Bologna, the Fat One." It was here that mortadella di Bologna (Italian spiced baloney) was invented, and any comparison between it and American baloney would be like comparing fresh ravioli with canned—it can't be done.

Northwest of Bologna is Parma, a picturesque medieval town known for its famous grating cheese, Parmesan, and prosciutto, the Italian ham that is the first choice of most Italian families.

Also in the Emilia-Romagna region is Ferrara, famed for its superb pannetone, a large Christmas sweet bread that is available almost anywhere. Pannetone is traditionally eaten on Christmas morning for breakfast but, frankly, it is delicious anytime.

As you embark upon your culinary journey, I wish you: *buon appetito!*

Aosta

Aosta is the capital of Valle d'Aosta and the site of winter sports. This dish is typical of the international influence on the cuisine of the region, which draws winter sports enthusiasts from all over the world.

Delicate Spaghetti
SPAGHETTI DELICATI

The delicate taste and aroma of salmon gives this dish its name. Food historians, by the way, tell us that Worcestershire sauce is the modern equivalent of *garum,* a fish sauce used in ancient Rome.

8 tablespoons butter

1 clove garlic, peeled and crushed

6 fresh sage leaves

1 pound fresh salmon, skinned, boned, washed, and cut into 1-inch strips

1 cup shelled roasted pistachio nuts, chopped

2 tablespoons unflavored brandy

1 pound spaghetti

2 dashes Worcestershire sauce

Juice of 1 lemon

Salt to taste

2 ounces smoked salmon, julienned

In a large skillet, melt butter over moderate heat. Add garlic and 3 of the sage leaves, and sauté for 3 minutes. Add fresh salmon strips and cook for 4 minutes.

Add pistachio nuts and brandy to the salmon, and cook over moderate heat for 5 minutes.

Cook pasta until al dente. Drain well and pour into the skillet containing the cooked salmon.

Sprinkle with Worcestershire sauce, lemon juice, and salt to taste. Toss well and pour into a serving bowl. Top with the smoked salmon strips and the rest of the sage leaves. Add salt. Serve immediately.

4 servings

Tricolored Spiral Pasta, Garden Style

PASTA AI TRICOLORI DELL'ORTO

A colorful repast that is a tribute to the red, white,
and green of Italy's flag.

½ pound package frozen artichoke
hearts, defrosted and chopped

1 medium onion, peeled and diced

2 tablespoons butter

4 tablespoons olive oil

2 bell peppers, 1 red, 1 green, washed,
seeded, and cut into strips

Salt and pepper to taste

10 pitted black olives, chopped

20 fresh basil leaves, chopped

½ pound fresh mushrooms, washed
and sliced

2 tablespoons fresh parsley, minced

1 pound tricolored spirals or white
corkscrew pasta

Bring a pot of water to a boil. Add salt and artichoke hearts, and boil for 10 minutes. Drain and chop. In a small frying pan, sauté the artichokes in 1 tablespoon butter for 5 minutes.

In a large saucepan, heat olive oil over medium heat and cook onion until soft and translucent. Add bell pepper strips and sauté for 10 minutes. Season the onion with salt and pepper. Add the cooked artichoke hearts, olives, and basil leaves, and simmer, covered, for 30 minutes.

In a small sauté pan, melt the remaining butter, add mushrooms and parsley, and sauté over medium heat for 20 minutes. Cook pasta until al dente, drain well.

When the pasta is cooled and drained, add it to the artichoke mixture and stir. Add the mushroom mixture and stir. Let the pasta heat through for a minute or so before transferring it to a serving bowl.

4 servings

Breuil-Cervinia

Breuil-Cervinia is a ski resort town high in the Italian Alps. It is cold here even on summer nights.

Stimulating Macaroni
PENNE STUZZICANTI

The recipe's name suggests that it acts as an aphrodisiac—or merely warms you up in a chilly climate.

1 large cauliflower, broken into florets

1 tablespoon salt

2 tablespoons butter

2 scallions, chopped

2 ounces bacon, chopped

1 package saffron, dissolved in
    1 tablespoon stock or water

2½ ounces pitted black olives,
    coarsely chopped

Salt and pepper to taste

1 pound penne or rigatoni

Grated Parmesan cheese

Bring water to a rolling boil in a large pot. Add cauliflower and 1 tablespoon salt, and boil for 10 minutes. Drain and set aside.

In a large skillet, melt butter over moderate heat. Add scallions and sauté until very lightly browned. Add chopped bacon, cook for 2 minutes. Add cauliflower and sauté for 2 minutes. Add saffron in stock. Cook for 3 minutes. Add olives, stir, and taste. If necessary, correct seasoning.

Cook pasta until al dente. Drain well. Pour into a serving bowl. Toss with the sauce, sprinkle with grated cheese, and bring to the table.

4 servings

Verrès

Egg Noodles in a Crown

TAGLIATELLE IN CORONA

A dramatic presentation that recalls the days
when Italy was a kingdom.

1 medium onion, peeled and minced

2 tablespoons olive oil

10 ounces frozen peas

½ chicken or beef bouillon cube

2 ounces prosciutto or boiled ham
in 2 slices

1 pound flat egg noodles

2 ounces mascarpone or cream cheese

2 egg yolks

Salt and pepper to taste

1 tablespoon unsalted butter

1½ ounces Romano cheese, shaved or
thinly sliced

In a large skillet, set over medium heat, sauté onion in olive oil until soft. Add frozen peas and cook for 5 minutes. Crumble bouillon cube over peas, cover, and simmer over low heat for 10 minutes. Slice ham into strips, add to peas, cover, and cook another 5 minutes.

In a warm bowl, beat mascarpone and egg yolks, and add salt and pepper.

Cook noodles in salted water until al dente. Drain pasta, reserving 2 tablespoons of the water. Toss with butter, cheese and egg yolk mixture, and reserved pasta water.

Pour noodle mixture in a buttered ring mold and let sit for 2 minutes. Unmold onto a warm serving dish. Pour pea mixture into the center of the pasta ring. Shave 1½ ounces of Romano cheese on top.

4 servings

Novara

Novara, beautifully situated in the foothills of the Alps, is the town where most fine Italian shoes are manufactured. It is also where mountain climbers prepare themselves for their exhilarating sport.

Mountain Climbers' Macaroni
PENNE DELL'ALPINO

Pasta from the Piemonte region—at the base of the Alps—provides a hearty, rich meal for mountain climbers. But this is a great winter dish for those of us living nearer to sea level. After this earthy dish you may well be tempted to go mountain climbing.

2 small eggplants, peeled, sliced into ¼-inch rounds, then julienned

2 medium zucchini, julienned

½ cup vegetable oil (for frying eggplant and zucchini)

4 tablespoons olive oil

1 scallion or green onion, chopped

1 large yellow bell pepper, seeded and julienned

1-pound can Italian peeled plum tomatoes, drained and chopped

2 ounces pitted black olives, diced

1 pound penne or rigatoni

1 pound mozzarella cheese, cubed

½ cup fresh basil leaves, chopped, or 1 teaspoon dried basil

1 clove garlic, peeled and crushed

Salt and pepper to taste

In a large, deep skillet, fry eggplant and zucchini in vegetable oil until lightly browned. Drain and place on paper towels to absorb oil.

In a large saucepan, heat the rest of the olive oil over medium heat. Sauté scallion and garlic until lightly browned. Add bell pepper and sauté for 5 minutes. Add chopped tomatoes and sauté over high heat for 3 minutes.

Reduce heat to medium, season with salt and pepper, and stir in sautéed eggplant and zucchini. Cook for 10 more minutes. Remove from heat and stir in black olives.

Cook pasta until al dente. Drain well and pour into sauce. Toss well. Transfer to serving bowl, add mozzarella and basil. Toss until mozzarella begins to melt, then serve.

4 servings

Large Ribbon Macaroni in Pheasant Sauce

PAPPARDELLE ALLA FARAONA

Pheasant is the traditional ingredient in this dish,
but you may substitute chicken.

1 medium onion, peeled and minced

5 thin slices or ¼ pound pancetta (Italian bacon), prosciutto (Italian ham), or boiled ham, minced

2 tablespoons olive oil

2 tablespoons fresh Italian (flat leaf) parsley or curly parsley, minced

2 pheasant drumsticks

Salt

½ cup dry white wine

10 ounces porcini mushrooms or any other strong mushroom, sliced into matchsticks

1 cup fresh chicken broth or bouillon

2 teaspoons tomato paste

Juice of 1 small lemon

Black pepper and grated Parmesan or Romano cheese to taste

1 pound pappardelle or flat lasagne (not ridged)

In a large skillet, sauté onion and ½ of pancetta in olive oil until they begin to turn golden brown. Add the parsley, the remaining pancetta, and the pheasant drumsticks, and brown over low heat about 10 minutes. Add salt and wine, and cook, uncovered, for 1 hour. Add more wine as needed so that the mixture does not burn.

When the pheasant sauce is 20 minutes from being done, add mushrooms. Then remove the drumsticks, debone them, and cut the meat into thin slices.

Return the meat to the pan, adding the chicken broth, tomato paste, and lemon juice. Simmer for 4 minutes. Cook pappardelle until al dente, and drain. Pour pasta into a large serving bowl and toss with sauce. Add 1 teaspoon or more freshly ground black pepper. Serve sprinkled with a generous amount of grated Parmesan or Romano cheese.

4 servings

Asti is the city that produces the Italian version of champagne, Asti Spumante, a delicately sweet bubbly wine that is often served on important occasions, such as weddings. It was here that I tasted this wonderful dish.

Crisped Angel Hair Pasta
CAPELLINI AU GRATIN

I suggest serving a simple green salad with this very rich dish.

4 scant tablespoons potato flour (ordinary flour will do as well)

2 cups milk

8 tablespoons butter, at room temperature

Nutmeg, salt, and pepper to taste

2 large eggs, at room temperature, separated

1 pound capellini or angel hair pasta

¼ cup grated Parmesan cheese

5 tablespoons heavy cream

¼ cup unseasoned bread crumbs

Preheat oven to 400°F.

In a large saucepan, over medium heat combine the flour with the milk, whisking continuously for 5 minutes. As the sauce thickens and begins to boil, add 3 tablespoons butter, a dash of nutmeg, and salt and pepper. Remove from the heat and allow to cool to room temperature, stirring the sauce occasionally.

In the meantime, put on the water for the pasta. A few minutes before cooking the pasta, add egg yolks to the lukewarm sauce. In a small bowl, beat egg whites with a dash of salt until stiff. Add to sauce.

Cook pasta in boiling water for 1 minute. Drain and pour into warmed bowl. Toss with 2 tablespoons of grated cheese and heavy cream, then pour into a buttered ovenproof dish and cover with sauce. Sprinkle with the rest of the grated cheese and the bread crumbs. Dot with the remaining butter. Bake for 20 minutes, until top is crusty brown. Serve immediately.

4 servings

Domodossola

Sharpshooters' Macaroni

PENNE AL BERSAGLIERE

This was traditionally served once a week in the military mess halls of the *bersaglieri,* the troops who have defended Italy's borders since 1870.

5 tablespoons olive oil

5 large cloves garlic, peeled and crushed

1 tablespoon hot pepper flakes

4 anchovy fillets, washed and minced

4 tablespoons unseasoned bread crumbs

1½ tablespoons capers, rinsed

4 tablespoons grated Pecorino Romano or Parmesan cheese

Salt and pepper to taste

4 drops Worcestershire sauce

1 pound penne or rigatoni

½ cup fresh parsley, minced

In a large skillet, heat olive oil over moderate heat. Add garlic and hot pepper, and sauté for 2 minutes. Add anchovies and stir until dissolved. Add bread crumbs, stir, increase heat to high, and cook until the mixture is light brown, about three minutes. Reduce heat to low and stir in capers, grated cheese, salt and pepper, and Worcestershire sauce. Remove from heat and set aside.

Cook pasta until al dente. Drain well and pour into a large skillet. Add sauce, toss, and sauté for 2 minutes. Pour into a warmed bowl, sprinkle with parsley, and serve.

4 servings

Penne with Cream of Basil Sauce

PENNE CON CREMA AL BASILICO

Try making this dish when pungent fresh basil is available from your garden or greenmarket.

2 tablespoons butter

2 tablespoons flour

2 cups milk

1 cup packed fresh basil leaves, minced

1 clove garlic, peeled and minced

Salt and pepper to taste

2 tablespoons grated Pecorino Romano cheese

2 tablespoons grated Parmesan cheese

1 pound penne or rigatoni

2 tablespoons unseasoned bread crumbs

Preheat oven to 350°F.

In a saucepan, melt butter over moderate heat. When butter has melted, whisk in flour, stirring constantly until butter is absorbed into the flour, about 2 minutes. Add milk and stir constantly until the sauce thickens, about 5 minutes. Add basil, garlic, salt and pepper, and grated cheeses. Set aside.

Cook pasta until al dente. Drain well and toss with basil sauce.

Butter an ovenproof baking dish and dust with bread crumbs. Add pasta and bake until a golden crust forms on top, about 20 minutes. Remove from oven and let stand for 5 minutes before serving.

4 servings

Pavia

At the center of medieval Pavia in Lombardia is the Certosa di Pavia, a huge monastery that used to house hundreds of Carthusian monks who belong to the severest order in the Catholic Church. They observe a vow of silence and are allowed to talk only once a year. The monks do very demanding physical labor, and often live to a ripe old age.

Penne with Leeks
PENNE CON PORRI

This dish comes from Pavia, the site of a large monastery. We know that this recipe does not come from the monks' kitchen because they never eat meat.

3 leeks, green tops removed, white bulbs trimmed, sliced lengthwise, and carefully washed

6 tablespoons extra-virgin olive oil

4 tablespoons butter

1 large onion, peeled and thinly sliced

5 ounces Italian sausage, skinned and crumbled

1 cup dry white wine

1 cup beef broth

Salt and pepper to taste

1½ pounds penne or rigatoni

¼ cup grated Parmesan cheese

Bring a pot of water to a boil, add leeks, boil for 1 minute, and drain.

Heat 3 tablespoons olive oil in a large saucepan with 2 tablespoons butter. Add onion and sauté until light brown.

Add sausage and cook for 5 minutes, stirring with a wooden spoon. Add wine, and cook over high heat until liquid has evaporated. Lower heat to medium, add beef broth, salt and pepper, and cook for 4 minutes. Stir in leeks and set aside.

Cook pasta until al dente. Drain well. Pour the pasta into the saucepan containing the sauce. Add the remaining olive oil, stir, and heat for 1 minute over moderate heat. Add the remaining butter and the grated cheese.

Pour into a bowl and serve.

4 servings

Milano

Milan-Style Pasta

PASTA ALLA MILANESE

A variation of Risotto Milanese, with pasta substituting for rice.

1 quart beef broth (you may use bouillon cubes)

4 tablespoons butter

½ large onion, peeled and thinly sliced

1 pound ditalini or any very short tubular pasta

2 small packages saffron

2 heaping tablespoons grated Parmesan cheese

In a saucepan, bring broth to a boil. In the meantime, melt 2 tablespoons butter in another saucepan, add the onion, and sauté until soft. Add the raw pasta and cook for 3 minutes, stirring with a wooden spoon.

When the broth has boiled, add 2 ladles of it to the pasta, add saffron, and cook over moderate heat until the pasta has absorbed the broth. Ladle more broth into the pasta and allow pasta to cook until al dente.

When pasta is done, remove from the heat, add remaining butter, sprinkle with cheese, pour into a warmed bowl, and serve.

4 servings

Harlequin Bow Ties

FARFALLE ARLECCHINO

A colorful combination of ingredients that recalls the traditional costume of the harlequin, the court jester or clown of medieval times.

2 tablespoons butter

3 tablespoons olive oil

2 yellow bell peppers, washed, seeded, and cut into thin strips

1 skinless chicken breast, trimmed of all fat and connective tissue, cut into thin strips

1 clove garlic, peeled and minced

1/4 cup dry white wine

4 Italian canned tomatoes, drained and coarsely chopped

Salt and pepper to taste

2 tablespoons minced fresh parsley, sage, and rosemary

1 cup beef or chicken stock (or bouillon)

12 ounces bow-tie pasta

In a large skillet, melt butter in olive oil over low heat.

Adjust heat to medium, add bell pepper strips and cook until soft. Add chicken and minced garlic and cook for 5 minutes. Add wine and cook until wine evaporates, about 5 minutes.

Add tomatoes, season with a dash of salt and pepper, add herbs and 1/2 cup stock. Cook over low heat for about 1/2 hour, adding more stock if sauce thickens too much.

In the meantime, cook pasta until al dente. Drain well, and stir into sauce. Cook 2 more minutes. Pour into a bowl and serve immediately.

4 servings

Genova

Flavorful Pasta

PASTA SAPORITA

I was able to spend only one day in Genoa, but the dining experience was so delightful that on my next trip to Italy, I plan to stay in Liguria longer!

4 tablespoons olive oil

½ large onion, peeled and thinly sliced

4 ounces lean ground beef

2 ounces Italian sausage, skinned and crumbled

4½ tablespoons dry white wine

Salt to taste

1 yellow bell pepper, seeded and cut into long strips

1 pound penne rigate or any short pasta

3 ounces mascarpone or cream cheese

¼ cup grated Parmesan or Pecorino Romano cheese

In a saucepan, heat 2 tablespoons olive oil over medium heat. Add onion and sauté until soft, not browned, about 5 minutes. Add beef and sausage, and stir constantly until meat is lightly browned. Add wine, a dash of salt, cover, and simmer over low heat for 35 minutes.

In the meantime, in a frying pan, sauté pepper strips in 2 tablespoons olive oil and a dash of salt until soft, about 10 minutes.

Cook pasta in salted water until al dente. Drain in a colander, saving ¼ cup pasta water. In a serving bowl, mix mascarpone or cream cheese with pasta water until blended. Add pasta and stir to coat evenly. Add meat sauce and yellow pepper strips, sprinkle with grated cheese, and serve.

4 servings

Penne, Provence Style

PENNE ALLA PROVENZALE

I have tasted—and enjoyed—this same recipe in Nice, France, and Ventimiglia, a reflection of the natural blend of two cultures and cuisines that are geographically virtually minutes apart.

1 tablespoon butter

2 tablespoons olive oil

1 large onion, peeled and diced

2 tablespoons dry white wine

1-pound can Italian peeled plum tomatoes, drained and chopped

1 chicken bouillon cube, crushed

2 ounces oil-cured black olives, pitted and halved

1 cup chopped fresh basil, sage, parsley, and oregano (if fresh aromatic herbs are unavailable, mix together 1 tablespoon dried basil, 1 tablespoon dried parsley, 1/2 teaspoon dry sage, and 1/2 teaspoon dry oregano)

1 pound penne or rigatoni

Salt and pepper to taste

1 tablespoon grated Parmesan cheese

In a large saucepan, melt butter and olive oil over moderate heat. Add sliced onions and allow to soften for 20 minutes, adding wine while the onions cook.

Add tomatoes, crushed bouillon cube, olives, and herbs. Stir and cook for 15 minutes over moderate heat.

Cook pasta until al dente, drain well, pour into a serving bowl, and toss with sauce. Add salt and pepper and grated cheese. Stir and serve.

4 servings

Rovigo
Large Shell Pasta with Zucchini
CONCHIGLIONI ALLE ZUCCHINE

Preparing these stuffed shells takes some time and effort.
The results, however, make it all worthwhile.

- 2 tablespoons olive oil
- 4 medium onions, peeled and thinly sliced
- 2 medium zucchini, washed and sliced into julienne (matchsticks)
- Salt and pepper to taste
- 6 tablespoons butter
- 2 tablespoons all-purpose flour
- 1 cup hot milk
- 2 ounces boiled ham, diced
- 4 ounces fontina, mild Provolone, or Swiss cheese, diced
- 1 scant tablespoon marjoram
- 12 ounces large pasta shells
- 4 ounces Asiago or Parmesan cheese, grated

In a large sauté pan, heat 1 tablespoon olive oil over a low flame. Add onions and sauté until they are just beginning to brown. Stir in the zucchini, add a dash of salt, and cook for 10 minutes.

Melt 2 tablespoons butter in a saucepan. Add flour and whisk until flour looks lightly toasted (roux). Add hot milk, a dash of salt, and whisk over low heat until thickened, about 10 minutes. Stir in diced ham, diced cheese, and marjoram, then add the sauce to the zucchini and onion mixture.

Cook pasta until al dente, drain well, and set aside to cool. With a teaspoon, fill each pasta shell with the zucchini sauce.

Preheat oven to 350°F.

Grease an ovenproof baking dish with 2 tablespoons butter. Place filled shells in pan, sprinkle with black pepper, the remaining butter, melted, and the grated cheeses. Bake for 20 minutes. Remove the shells from the oven and let stand, covered, for 5 minutes before serving.

4 servings

Perfumed Linguine

LINGUINE PROFUMATI

The wonderful aroma of fresh herbs give this recipe its title.

1 pound linguine

4 tablespoons olive oil

1 tablespoon minced chives

1 tablespoon minced fresh thyme, or
  1/4 teaspoon dried thyme

1 tablespoon chopped fresh parsley

1 clove garlic, peeled and crushed

3 medium zucchini, julienned

Salt and pepper to taste

1/2 pound smoked or fresh mozzarella
  cheese, cubed

Cook pasta until al dente. Drain and rinse quickly under cold water. Pour into a bowl and dress with 2 tablespoons olive oil and the chives, thyme, and parsley.

In a skillet, heat 2 tablespoons olive oil. Add garlic and sauté over moderate heat for 1 minute. Add zucchini and, over high heat, sauté until still crisp, 4 minutes maximum.

Salt zucchini to taste and remove from heat. Toss with pasta, along with mozzarella and black pepper to taste. Return to skillet, and heat over a low flame for a minute or two. Pour into a bowl and serve.

4 servings

Rigatoni in an Unusual Style

RIGATONI ALLA MODA INSOLITA

Traditionally, rigatoni is served with a thick meat or tomato sauce. But this flavorful exception is studded with vegetables, tuna, capers, and olive paste for a robust-tasting treat.

4 tablespoons olive oil

2 leeks, greens tops removed, bulbs trimmed and minced

1 stalk celery, minced

2 scallions, minced

2 heads red radicchio, julienned

2 ounces bacon, minced

1 small onion, peeled and minced

1 6½-ounce can tuna packed in oil, drained and flaked

1 tablespoon capers, rinsed

2 tablespoons black olive paste (available in specialty food shops)

2 tablespoons dry white wine

1 tablespoon butter, at room temperature

1 pound rigatoni

Salt and pepper to taste

2 fresh sage leaves

In a large skillet, heat olive oil over moderate heat. Add leeks, celery, scallions, radicchio, bacon, and onion. Cook over the lowest possible heat for 15 minutes. Add flaked tuna, capers, and olive paste.

Adjust heat to high, add wine and cook briskly for 2 minutes. Remove from heat, add butter and beat the sauce with a fork to amalgamate all ingredients. Set aside.

Cook pasta until al dente and drain well. Pour into the skillet with the sauce and mix well. Add salt and pepper and sage leaves. Transfer to a warmed bowl and serve.

4 servings

Treviso, a lovely medieval town near Venice, is famous for its radicchio, a red and white bitter lettuce that is increasingly popular in the United States.

Treviso Pasta au Gratin

PENNE DI TREVISO GRATINATE

Radicchio has a distinctively bitter but pleasant taste. If you cannot find it in your local shops, you may substitute the outer green leaves of romaine lettuce. I have tried it in this recipe when radicchio was not available. It works very well. Two cups of chopped romaine will be enough for the recipe.

2 tablespoons butter

2 tablespoons olive oil

1 clove garlic, peeled and crushed

4 anchovy fillets, rinsed and minced

4 heads fresh red radicchio, coarsely chopped

Salt and pepper to taste

2 drops Worcestershire sauce

2 tablespoons heavy cream

1 pound penne or rigatoni

2 tablespoons grated Parmesan cheese

2 tablespoons unseasoned bread crumbs

Melt butter and olive oil in a large skillet over moderate heat. Add garlic and anchovies, and sauté until anchovies dissolve. Add radicchio, adjust heat to high, stir, and cook for 2 minutes. Lower heat to moderate, season with salt and pepper and Worcestershire sauce. Add heavy cream, stir, and cook for 2 more minutes. Set aside.

Cook pasta until al dente. Drain well. Pour directly into the skillet containing the sauce, toss, and sprinkle with grated cheese.

Preheat oven to 350°F.

Pour pasta and sauce into an ovenproof dish. Sprinkle with bread crumbs and dot with butter. Bake for 5 minutes, or until butter has melted. Serve.

4 servings

Gorizia

Gorizia is provincial capital of the area and is as charming as its bustling population. I made some great friends here. Because of Gorizia's proximity of Slovenia, both Slovenian and Italian languages are spoken here.

Linguine with Crabmeat
LINGUINE AL GRANCHIO

Y ou may want to try scallops or shrimp instead of crabmeat in this dish.

3 tablespoons olive oil

3 large cloves garlic, peeled and crushed

1 small red bell pepper, seeded and julienned

1 small yellow pepper, seeded and julienned

5 ounces canned crabmeat (or frozen, defrosted), drained and cut into chunks

2 tablespoons unflavored brandy

½ cup dry white wine

Salt and pepper to taste

1 tablespoon minced fresh parsley

1 pound linguine

In a large skillet, heat olive oil over moderate heat. Add garlic and cook until golden (do not brown). Add julienned bell peppers and cook for 10 minutes. Add crabmeat, sprinkle with brandy, and cook for 2 minutes. Add wine and salt and pepper. Remove from heat, stir in parsley, and set aside.

Cook pasta until al dente. Drain well. Pour into the skillet with the sauce, toss gently, and sauté over moderate heat for 2 minutes. Pour into a warmed bowl, garnish with more fresh parsley, and serve.

4 servings

Fusilli from the Garden and the Sea
FUSILLI ORTO MARE

This delicious combination of vegetables and fish in a creamy sauce, unusual in Italian fare, reflects the Slavic influence in northern Italy.

2 tablespoons olive oil

1 tablespoon butter

1 small onion, peeled and sliced

1 heart of lettuce, washed and cut into strips

1 8-ounce can peas, drained

Salt and pepper to taste

¼ cup beef or chicken stock

3 canned boneless mackerel fillets or canned boneless sardines, drained

1 tablespoon chopped fresh parsley

¼ cup Bechamel Sauce (page 4)

1 pound fusilli or any corkscrew pasta

2 tablespoons grated Parmesan cheese

Melt oil and butter in a large saucepan over low heat. When butter has melted, add onion and sauté until lightly browned. Add lettuce and peas. Stir, add salt and pepper, and simmer for 1 minute. Add stock and continue simmering for 15 minutes.

Cut mackerel or sardines into small pieces, add to sauce along with parsley and half of the bechamel sauce. Set aside.

Preheat oven to 450°F.

Cook pasta until al dente. Drain well and pour into sauce, toss gently. Transfer to a buttered ovenproof dish. Cover with the remainder of the bechamel, grated cheese, and a sprinkle of chopped parsley. Bake for 5 minutes, or until cheese has begun to melt. Remove from oven and let stand for 5 minutes before serving.

4 servings

Bolzano
Egg Noodles of the Forest
TAGLIATELLE DEL BOSCO

The paprika and yogurt in this otherwise typically Italian recipe recall
the time when northeastern Italy was part of
the Austro-Hungarian empire.

4 tablespoons olive oil

3 large bell peppers, 1 yellow, 2 red,
  seeded and julienned

1 clove garlic, peeled and crushed

2 leeks, green tops removed, white
  bulbs trimmed, sliced lengthwise and
  carefully washed, then sliced
  paper thin

1/4 cup canned tomato sauce

1 ounce dried mushrooms, softened in
  1 cup lukewarm water, drained
  through cheesecloth, and chopped

1/4 cup plain yogurt

2 tablespoons chopped fresh parsley

1 teaspoon paprika

1 pound flat egg noodles

1/4 cup grated Parmesan cheese

Heat 2 tablespoons olive oil in a large saucepan over moderate heat. Add
bell pepper strips, leeks, garlic, and tomato sauce, and sauté for 10 minutes.
Set aside to cool.

In the meantime, sauté mushrooms in remaining 2 tablespoons olive oil
over moderate heat for 5 minutes. Place tomato sauce into the bowl of a food
processor fitted with the steel knife blade. Add yogurt, parsley, and paprika
and process for 1 minute. Return to saucepan. Add mushrooms and salt and
pepper to the sauce and cook over moderate heat for 5 minutes.

Cook pasta until al dente, drain well, pour into a pasta bowl. Toss the
sauce with the pasta and top with grated cheese. Serve.

4 servings

Shells with Grapes

CONCHIGLIE ALL'UVA

I first encountered this unusual—and refreshing—pasta dish in Trento.

¼ pound butter

1 large onion, peeled and diced

Salt and pepper to taste

7 ounces boiled ham, diced

20 large white seedless grapes

1 cup dry white wine

¼ teaspoon dried marjoram

¼ teaspoon chives

1 pound medium pasta shells

¼ cup grated Parmesan cheese

In a large saucepan, melt butter over low heat. Add onion and cook until onion is soft and translucent. Stir and add pepper. Add diced ham and cook for 5 minutes.

Stir grapes and wine into the sauce and cook until wine evaporates, about 5 minutes. Add marjoram and chives, and salt and pepper to taste, and cook over low heat for 20 minutes.

Cook pasta until al dente. Drain and pour into a serving bowl. Toss sauce with pasta and top with a sprinkle of grated Parmesan cheese. Serve.

4 servings

Ferrara

Bow-Tie Pasta with Fried Egg Ribbons and Peas

FARFALLE CON LISTARELLI DI FRITTATA E PISELLI

The egg ribbons are a distinctive addition to this wonderful one-dish meal.

3 tablespoons butter

1 slice boiled ham (weighing about 1½ ounces), chopped

½ medium white onion, peeled and finely diced

10 ounces frozen peas

Salt and pepper to taste

1 tablespoon chopped fresh parsley

2 large eggs

2 tablespoons milk

6 tablespoons grated Parmesan cheese

1 tablespoon heavy cream

1 pound bow-tie pasta

In a small skillet, melt 1½ tablespoons butter over moderate heat. Add ham and onion and sauté until onion is soft and translucent. Add peas and cover and simmer for 20 minutes. Add salt and pepper and parsley.

In a bowl, beat eggs with milk, 2 tablespoons grated cheese, cream, and a pinch of salt. Set aside. In a 12-inch nonstick skillet, melt the remaining butter over moderate heat. Pour in egg mixture and cook until set well, about 10 minutes. The bottom should be lightly browned. Set aside to cool. When the frittata is cool, remove from pan, roll tightly into a cylinder, and slice into thin strips.

Cook pasta until al dente. Drain well and pour into a serving bowl. Toss pasta with the sauce. Add fried egg strips. Sprinkle with the remaining cheese, dot with butter, and you are ready to serve.

4 servings

Modena

Modena is the home of balsamic vinegar. And it is the hometown, too, of the great operatic tenor Luciano Pavarotti, who started his career singing in the church choir here; his father was the choirmaster.

Bow Ties with Shrimp

FARFALLE AI GAMBERI

Delicate shrimp and tangy eggplant create
a symphony of color and taste.

- 4 tablespoons olive oil
- I scallion or spring onion, diced
- 2 bay leaves, whole
- 2-ounce slice Canadian bacon, diced
- I chicken bouillon cube, crushed
- 2 small eggplants, I peeled,
    I unpeeled, diced
- ¼ cup cognac or unflavored brandy
- Salt and pepper to taste
- 12 large frozen shrimp, deveined
- I pound bow-tie pasta
- 2 tablespoons chopped fresh parsley

In a large skillet, heat 2 tablespoons oil over moderate heat. Add scallion, bay leaves, Canadian bacon, bouillon cube, and eggplant, and cook for 5 minutes. Add 2 tablespoons of the cognac, salt, and cook for 3 minutes. Remove from heat and set aside.

In another skillet, heat the remaining 2 tablespoons olive oil until very hot. Add shrimp and sauté for 2 minutes, or until shrimp turn pink. Add the remaining cognac, salt and pepper and remove from heat.

Add the shrimp to the eggplant, stir, and simmer for 10 minutes, or until the eggplant is translucent.

Cook pasta until al dente. Drain well and add to sauce. Stir and simmer for 2 minutes. Pour into a serving bowl, sprinkle with fresh chopped parsley, and serve.

4 servings

Penne with Eggplant and Walnuts

PENNE CON MELANZANE E NOCI

The mixture of pesto and ricotta makes an especially rich and satisfying sauce.

½ cup vegetable oil (for frying eggplant)

2 medium eggplants, peeled and julienned

32 walnut halves, coarsely chopped

1 clove garlic, peeled

½ cup fresh basil leaves

½ cup ricotta cheese

2 tablespoons grated sharp Pecorino Romano or Parmesan cheese

3 tablespoons extra-virgin olive oil

2 tablespoons hot water or pasta water

1 pound penne or rigatoni

Salt and pepper

Preheat oven to 200°F.

Heat vegetable oil in a deep skillet over moderate heat until very hot. Add the eggplant and fry 4 or 5 minutes until browned. Remove the eggplant, using a slotted spoon, and blot on paper towels. Place in oven to keep warm.

In a food processor fitted with the metal blade, place walnuts, garlic, basil leaves, ricotta, and grated cheese. Process for 1 minute. Carefully remove metal blade and replace with plastic blade. Process with a few pulses, adding olive oil and 2 tablespoons hot water. Set aside.

Cook pasta until al dente. Drain well. Pour into a serving bowl. Toss with sauce and eggplant, and season to taste. Serve immediately.

4 servings

Mediterranean Macaroni

PASTA MEDITERRANEA

This dish, native to Bologna, is curiously named, given that its place of origin is a landlocked city that is virtually equidistant from the two coasts of Italy.

7 ounces ground veal

2 ounces boiled ham, minced

2 egg yolks

2 tablespoons minced fresh parsley

½ ounce grated Parmesan cheese

Salt and pepper to taste

1 tablespoon all-purpose flour

1 tablespoon butter

2 scallions or spring onions, bulbs peeled and minced

1 28-ounce can Italian peeled plum tomatoes, drained and coarsely chopped

1 tablespoon heavy cream

1 pound penne rigate pasta

Preheat oven to 350°F.

In a mixing bowl, place veal, ham, egg yolks, parsley, cheese, and salt and pepper. Mix well and form into small meatballs. Dust each meatball lightly with flour then roll in a plate of flour. Coat a cookie sheet lightly with oil, and place meatballs on sheet. Bake for 10 minutes. Remove from oven and set aside.

Melt butter in a small saucepan, add scallions and sauté until soft, about 5 minutes. Add tomatoes, stir, and cook over medium heat for 3 minutes. Stir in cream and salt and pepper, and cook over low heat for 15 minutes. Add meatballs, stir, and remove sauce from heat.

Cook pasta until al dente. Drain well and toss with sauce. Serve.

4 servings

Local Wines and Restaurants

Some restaurants where foods typical of the regions can be tasted and regional wines can be sampled:

Region	City	Restaurant
Valle d'Aosta	Aosta	Cavallo Bianco Via Aubert, 15

Cavallo Bianco is one of the oldest restaurants of Italy, and probably one of the better ones for genuine regional dishes. Four centuries ago the restaurant was an inn where the traveler could eat while waiting for a change of horses (*cavallo* means "horse" in Italian). The same soups and roasts that appeared on the menu then are still available today.

Some of the better known wines of Valle d'Aosta:

Blanc de Valdigne (dry white)

Pinot Gris (dry and sweet white)

Pinot Noir (dry red)

Vien de Nus (dry red)

The Italian government has established certain wines of every region as DOC. The initials stand for *Denominazione di Origine Controllata*, meaning Determination of Origin under Control. DOC wines are guaranteed to be made using the grapes of a particular region under strictly controlled conditions, which ensures their purity and authenticity.

The Italians are as serious about their wines as the French. In ancient times, the Greeks called Italy *Enotria*, which means the land of grapes and wine.

The DOC Wines of Valle d'Aosta

Donnaz
Enfer d'Arvier

Good non-DOC table wines include:

Aymavilles (dry red)
Blanc de Morgex (dry white)
Chambave Rouge (dry red)
Malvoisie de Nus (sweet dessert wine)
Passito di Chambave (sweet white)
Petit Rouge (dry red)
Riesling de Mont Cenis (dry white)
Sang des Salasses (dry red)
Torrette (quality dry red)
Vin du Conseil (dry white)

Region	City	Restaurant
Piemonte	Alessandria	Ristorante dell' Hotel Napoleon
		Via Circonvallazione Nuova, 1

The elegant and comfortable Ristorante dell' Hotel Napoleon is very near the Museum of the Battle of Marengo. It was during this battle that Napoleon's Italian chef invented the now famous recipe for Chicken Marengo. This restaurant's menu offers authentic dishes of Piemonte.

Some DOC Wines of Piemonte

The fine red wines listed here are the most popular, but there are twenty-seven more DOC wines of Piemonte.

Barbaresco

Barolo

Carema

Gattinara

Ghemme

Lessona

Nebbiolo d'Alba

The best Italian vermouths are also produced in this region.

Region	City	Restaurant
Lombardia	Pavia	Chalet della Certosa
		Piazzale Monumento, 1

A charming chalet in a beautiful forest setting, Chalet della Certosa serves the highest-quality authentic Lombardian dishes.

Some DOC Wines of Lombardia

These are the more popular dry red DOC wines:

Barbacarlo

Barbera

Bonarda

Botticino da Barbera

Buttafuoco

Marzemino

Merlot

Nebbiolo

Sangiovese

Sangue di Giuda

Schiava

Sfurzat

Valtellina

Recommended Non-DOC wines include:

Clastidium

Gaggiarone Amaro

Müller Thurgau

Region	City	Restaurant
Liguria	Genova	Antica Osteria Pacetti Borgo Incrociati, 22R

Until 1908, Antica Osteria Pacetti was a true osteria, a place where only wine was sold. Then it became a trattoria—serving an inexpensive Italian version of fast food—and subsequently became a restaurant. In Italy a restaurant is where you go to enjoy excellent food and wine and where you are pampered by elegant service. You can be assured the food here is authentically Ligurian.

Some DOC Wines of Liguria

Cinqueterre (dry white)
Cinqueterre Sciacchetrà (dessert wine)
Rossese di Dolceacqua (dry red)

Good non-DOC table wines include:

Pigato Bianco Secco (dry white)
Vermentino (dry white)

Region	City	Restaurant
Veneto	Venezia	Antica Bessetta Calle Salvio, 1395

With the mother cooking in the kitchen, and the father and son taking care of the dining room, Antica Bessetta is a simple, low-key place to enjoy what is no doubt the best of authentic Venetian cuisine.

The DOC Wines of Veneto

There are over fifty DOC wines, so here are just a few:

Bardolino (red and pink)

Bianco di Custoza (dry white)

Breganze (seven subdivisions) (red and white)

Gambellara (dry white and sweet)

Prosecco (sparkling dry, semidry, and sweet)

Soave (dry white)

Tocai Italico (white)

Valpolicella (red)

Good non-DOC table wines include:

Castello di Roncade (dry red)

Durello (dry white and sparkling)

Raboso (dry red)

Venegazzù della Casa (exceptionally good red)

Region	City	Restaurant
Friuli-Venezia Giulia	Udine	Alla Vedova
		Via Tavagnacco, 9

Situated on the outskirts of the city, Alla Vedova is one of the oldest restaurants in Udine and the one which, perhaps more than any other, captures the spirit of the region.

The DOC Wines of Friuli-Venezia Giulia

There are over forty wines in this classification, so I will name just a few:

Cabernet Sauvignon (dry red)
Carso Terrano (dry red)
Malvasia (dry white)
Merlot (smooth dry red)
Refosco (dry red)
Ribolla (dry white)
Riesling Italico (dry to off-dry white)
Tocai Friulano (dry white)
Verduzzo (dry and sweet)

Good non-DOC tables wines include:

Müller Thurgau di Latisana
Tunina nel Collio

Region	City	Restaurant
Trentino-Alto Adige	Bolzano	Moritzingerhof Via Merano, 113

Moritzingerhof, a restaurant of rigorous tradition, is an ideal place to taste the authentic dishes of the region. It is owned and operated by a hospitable and fascinating family headed by the papa, Franz Asper, who cooks with the help of his son Günter. One of their specialties, Strangolapreti, "Choke the Priest," is a pasta dish that can be found throughout Italy under similar names. The legend attending this dish goes something like this: The fat parish priest is always looking for a free meal. One of his parishioners, a housewife tired of the priest's demands, makes him a dish of homemade pasta that is so delicious that he almost vacuums it down his throat. It chokes him, and he dies. (The story reflects the sometimes not so subtle, but understandable, anticlericalism common to Catholic countries.)

The DOC Wines of Trentino-Alto Adige

Lagrein (red and pink)

Goldenmuskateller (sweet dessert wine)

Rosenmuskateller (fruity pink)

Weisburgunder (dry white)

Ruländer (dry white)

Welschriesling (dry white)

Sylvaner (dry white)

Traminer Aromatico (spicy dry white)

Veltliner (light dry white)

Most of the house wines are robust and good.

Region	City	Restaurant
Emilia-Romagna	Bologna	Cordon Bleu
		Via Aurelio Saffi, 38

The chef at Cordon Bleu is Pierantonio Zarotti, famous in the culinary world for his skill with both the traditional dishes of the region and the aristocratic cuisine of the wealthy. At this first-class restaurant, the dishes are as authentic as they can get.

The DOC Wines of Emilia-Romagna

Albana di Romagna (dry white, also available sweet)

Bianco di Scandiano (dry, semisweet, and sparkling white)

Lambrusco Grasparossa di Castelvetro (dry to sparkling red)

Lambrusco Reggiano (sparkling red)

Lambrusco Salamino di Santa Croce (dry or sweet sparkling red)

Malvasia dei Colli di Parma (dry, sweet, semisweet, and sparkling white)

Sauvignon dei Colli Bolognese (dry white)

For some time Lambrusco was "in." Although it's not "in" anymore, it is still a good wine.

Chapter 2

The Rich Cuisine
of
Central Italy

This region of Italy features a varied terrain and climate, where olive trees grow alongside grapevines. The cuisines of central Italy are full of strong flavors, and you'll find some of the world's most distinctive olive oil and wine here. The prosciutto is much stronger and saltier than that of other regions, and the sausages more highly flavored. Sauces for meats and stews are extremely spicy, providing the perfect accompaniment for the myriad pastas that grace the tables of central Italy.

Toscana (Tuscany) has not only given the world superb fare, but has also given Italy its official language. In 1870, in the kingdom of Italy it was debated which "dialect" would become the official national language, Tuscan (based on Latin) or Sicilian (based on Greek). After long and serious discussion, Tuscan was adopted as the national language.

Enduringly beautiful Firenze (Florence), home of Dante Alighieri, father of the Italian language and author of *The Divine Comedy*, is located in Tuscany. This is also where the exemplary Renaissance man Leonardo da Vinci lived and worked. It was here also that Michelangelo, the greatest sculptor of the world, learned his art (and I am sure you will agree that no one has yet even come close to the genius of his fine Italian hand).

Pitigliano (once known as "Little Jerusalem") is an ancient medieval town located in the lovely hills of Tuscany. It was an almost totally Jewish Italian town since A.D. 1100. In researching the history of Pitigliano, I discovered that the Jews had been protected from persecution for centuries because the town belonged to the powerful Orsini family, who apparently appreciated Jewish culture and tradition. (Of course, as a result of Italy's alliance with Nazi Germany during World War II, most of the Jews fled to other parts of Italy where they were protected by Catholics who opposed Nazi anti-Semitism.)

Just to the east of Toscana is *Umbria,* a region of dense forests that takes its name from the Latin word for dark or shadowy *(umbra).* The region's most notable cities are Perugia, the delectable chocolate capital of Italy, and Assisi, the home Saint Francis, the saint who is probably the most beloved in the Christian world. Spoleto, a small town in the Umbrian hills, would be just another medieval town were it not for Gian Carlo Menotti, the composer of modern operas, such as *Ahmal and the Night Visitors*. Once a year Spoleto is inundated with music lovers who come to attend the "Music Festival of the Two Worlds." Menotti, of course, is the impresario of the event.

Marche is the region that I firmly believe gives us some of the best cooking in Italy. From Ancona come some creative, imaginative fish and seafood meals, and Ascoli Piceno is notable for its deliciously rich pasta dishes. Among its many other interesting towns is Pesaro, this area's most important seaport; here, a lovely beach draws tourists from northern Europe who incidentally also enjoy a very fine regional cuisine.

The region of *Lazio* claims Rome, the Eternal City whose heritage is a marvelous combination of historic accuracy and mythic legend. And I can tell you that to dine in Rome is to enjoy an incomparable cuisine, with a variety that will astound—and delight—even the most discriminating visitor.

Not far from Rome is the seaside resort of Anzio, the town best remembered for the terrible loss of American soldiers' lives during World War II in a battle that marked the beginning of the end of the war in Europe. Also along the coast is Ostia, the port city of the Roman empire. In ancient times the Romans sailed down the Tiber River to Ostia, on the way to their far-flung conquests. It is now a seaside resort.

Adjacent to Lazio is *Abruzzi*, a land of legendary cuisine where some of the finest wheat in Italy is grown to produce the most flavorful pastas. It is also home to the mountain resort of Aquila, a charming and attractive capital city, and to Pescara, on the Adriatic, which boasts some of the best seafood along the shoreline.

I raise my wineglass to you with the traditional Italian toast: *cincin!*

Firenze

Flavorful Egg Noodles

TAGLIATELLE SAPORITE

A hearty dish, because it includes beans, a tasty one, because it has sausage in it.

1 tablespoon unsalted butter	Salt and pepper to taste
3 tablespoons olive oil	1 pint chicken or beef broth
1 medium carrot, peeled and diced	2 tablespoons canned tomato sauce
1 stalk celery, diced	1 pound flat egg noodles
1 small onion, peeled and diced	Grated Parmesan or Pecorino Romano cheese
½ pound Italian sausage, skinned and crumbled	
½ pound borlotti or pinto beans, soaked overnight, rinsed, and drained	

In a large skillet, melt butter and olive oil over medium heat. Lower heat to a simmer and add carrot, celery, onion, and sausage; cook for 5 to 6 minutes, stirring occasionally. Add beans, a dash of salt, and cover and simmer for 5 minutes. Add half of the broth and cook, uncovered, for another 5 minutes.

Stir in the tomato sauce, cover, and simmer over very low heat for about 1½ hours. As the beans cook, stir in the broth a little at a time as the cooking liquid evaporates. At the end, the sauce should be quite thick.

Cook the pasta in boiling salted water until al dente. Drain quickly in a colander, saving ¼ cup of the cooking water. Add the pasta to the sauce, stir, and sprinkle with coarse black pepper. Pour into a bowl, add the cooking water, and sprinkle generously with grated cheese before serving.

4 servings

Lucca

Lucca is a charming town that is close to the hearts of all cooks because it produces some of the finest olive oil in the world.

Exotic Pasta

PENNE ESOTICHE

An appropriate name for an Italian pasta dish that contains pineapple! This fruit does indeed add a special, unusual and, yes, exotic flavor to the meal.

1 tablespoon butter

3 tablespoons olive oil

1 large onion, peeled and sliced very thin

1 large red bell pepper, seeded and cut into strips

2 ounces pancetta, prosciutto, or boiled ham, diced

½ cup diced pineapple, drained

Salt

Powdered cayenne pepper

2 large eggs

1 tablespoon butter, melted

1 pound penne

In a 12-inch skillet (preferably nonstick), melt 1 tablespoon butter and 2 tablespoons olive oil over low heat. Add onion, bell pepper strips and pancetta, and brown lightly for 5 to 6 minutes. Add pineapple, a dash of salt, and a dash of cayenne pepper. Remove from heat, but cover to keep warm.

In the same skillet, heat 1 tablespoon olive oil. In a small bowl, beat eggs, adding a dash of salt and the melted butter. Pour eggs into skillet and fry until lightly brown on both sides and thoroughly cooked. Roll crepe into a tight cylinder, cut it into strips, add them to the sauce, and cover to keep warm.

Cook pasta until al dente, drain well, saving ¼ cup of the pasta water. Toss pasta in the skillet with the sauce. Add pasta water, toss again lightly, and warm for 2 minutes over medium heat. Pour into a pasta bowl and serve immediately.

4 servings

In keeping with the Italo-Jewish tradition of the ancient town of Pitigliano (Little Jerusalem), this recipe and the one that follows are kosher style—and thoroughly Italian.

Purim Ravioli

RAVIOLI DI PURIM

Purim is a joyful Jewish holiday during which children
dress in costume to celebrate.

2 pounds fresh spinach

2 tablespoons olive oil

I small onion, peeled and quartered

I small carrot, peeled and coarsely chopped

½ chicken breast, cubed

I teaspoon salt

⅛ teaspoon freshly ground black pepper to taste

I tablespoon flour

I recipe Homemade Pasta (page 4)

6 quarts water (to cook ravioli)

3 cups Basic Tomato Sauce (page 3)

To prepare spinach: Wash spinach well and place in pot with no extra water. Add a pinch of salt and cook, covered, for 5 minutes. Drain in a colander.

To make filling: Place oil, onion, carrot, and chicken breast in a large skillet. Add salt and pepper, and cook over moderate heat for 5 minutes, stirring frequently. Add drained spinach and cook, stirring, 5 more minutes, or until most of the liquid has evaporated. Add flour and cook for another minute, stirring constantly. Remove from heat, cool, then chop the mixture very fine.

To make ravioli: Roll out half of the pasta dough paper thin and place on floured cloth. Lightly brush surface of dough with cold water. Place small mounds of filling on dough about 2 inches apart (measurements are from center of mounds). You should have 8 or 9 dozen mounds when you're done.

Roll out the other half of dough paper thin and place loosely over the first sheet. Using your fingers, press dough around the mounds to form ravioli. With a fluted pastry wheel, press along the furrows, cutting and sealing at the same time.

Bring a pot of water to a rolling boil. Add ravioli and 3 tablespoons of salt. Stir until boiling resumes. Cook the ravioli for 4 to 5 minutes. Remove with a slotted spoon and drain well. Transfer to a bowl, toss with tomato sauce, and serve.

6 servings

Crusty Fettuccine Pharaoh's Wheel

COLLA CROCIA RUOTA DI FARAONE

The recipe is a bittersweet reminder of the Jews' enslavement in Egypt. Its name refers to the story in Exodus of how Pharaoh's chariots were trapped in the Red Sea.

1 recipe Homemade Pasta (page 4)

6 quarts water (to cook fettuccine)

3 cups Basic Tomato Sauce with meat (page 3)

½ cup diced kosher beef salami

¼ cup margarine

½ cup dark seedless raisins

½ cup whole shelled almonds

½ cup pignoli (pine nuts)

Preheat oven to 350°F.

Roll out dough to ⅛-inch thickness and form into a jelly roll, 2½ inches wide. Cut dough into ⅛-inch slices and toss to unfold noodles. Cook noodles in boiling water for 1 minute. Drain well.

Pour pasta into a large bowl with meat sauce and diced salami. Toss quickly to distribute sauce evenly.

In a bowl, mix the margarine, raisins, almonds, and pignoli until well blended.

In a well-greased ovenproof dish, pour in a layer of noodles, then a layer of nut and raisin mix, alternating until both are used up. Bake for 1 to 1½ hours, or until a nice crust is formed. Invert onto a platter and serve.

6 servings

Spoleto

Rigatoni Ready When the Pot Whistles

RIGATONI AL FISCHIO

The ancient and modern come together in this recipe. I first ate this superb dish in the ancient city of Spoleto and, as you will note, it takes advantage of a modern convenience, the pressure cooker.

1 tablespoon butter	Salt and pepper to taste
1 small onion, peeled and diced	½ cup beef broth
½ pound lean ground beef	1 bay leaf
1 link Italian sausage, skinned and crumbled	1 pound rigatoni
1-pound can crushed Italian plum tomatoes	Grated Parmesan cheese

Melt butter in a pressure cooker, add onion, and sauté over low heat until soft. Adjust heat to moderate, add ground beef and sausage, and cook, stirring, until meat is browned. Add tomatoes, salt and pepper, and cook over moderate heat for 10 minutes.

Add beef broth, bring to a boil. When the mixture boils, add bay leaf and pasta, stir well, and lock on cover. When the pot begins to "whistle," lower the heat and cook for 5 minutes. Carefully remove the cover. If there is any excess liquid, let the pasta sit, uncovered, until liquid is absorbed.

Pour the contents into a serving bowl, sprinkle with grated cheese, and serve.

4 servings

Terni

This was a never-to-be-forgotten dining experience in Terni, a small town near the spectacular waterfalls of Marmore.

Macaroni from Umbria
PENNE DELL'UMBRIA

I love the contrast of the tooth-tender pasta and the crunchy fried zucchini and onion.

2 eggs, separated

3 tablespoons yellow cornmeal

½ cup warm beer

1 tablespoon milk

Salt and pepper to taste

1 cup vegetable oil (for frying)

1 pound small zucchini, sliced into rounds

2 large onions, peeled and sliced into rings

1 pound penne or rigatoni

2 tablespoons olive oil

2 tablespoons grated Pecorino Romano or Parmesan cheese

8 fresh basil leaves, chopped

In a bowl, beat egg whites until very stiff but not dry. In a separate bowl, beat the egg yolks with cornmeal. Gradually add beer, milk, a dash of salt, and the egg whites.

Heat vegetable oil in a deep skillet or deep fryer until very hot. Dip zucchini rounds and onion rings into the egg batter. Fry them until golden brown and drain on paper towels. (You may keep them warm in a 200°F. oven.)

Cook pasta until al dente. Drain quickly, reserving 1 cup of the pasta water. Pour the pasta into a serving dish, and toss with olive oil, grated cheese, basil, pasta water, and salt and pepper. Add fried zucchini and onion, toss, and serve immediately.

4 servings

Rustic Rigatoni

RIGATONI RUSTICI

One can almost taste the flavors of the rustic hills of Umbria
in this pleasing, well-named dish.

1 tablespoon butter

2 tablespoons olive oil

1 clove garlic, peeled and minced

1 tablespoon minced fresh parsley

2 fresh sage leaves (if unavailable, omit
and double the amount of parsley)

3½ ounces or one link Italian sausage,
skinned and crumbled

1 6½-ounce can tuna fish packed in
oil, drained and flaked

½ cup dry white wine

1 cup beef broth, hot

1 tablespoon tomato paste

¼ cup canned white beans, drained

1 pound rigatoni

Grated Parmesan cheese

In a saucepan, melt butter and olive oil. Add garlic, parsley, and sage.
When garlic begins to brown, add sausage and cook for 10 minutes over
medium heat. Add tuna, cook for 5 minutes more, add wine, and continue
cooking until wine evaporates. Mix the beef broth with the tomato paste, and
stir into sauce. Bring to a slow boil and allow to cook, semicovered, for 25
minutes. Add beans and cook 5 minutes more. Remove from heat.

Cook pasta until al dente. Drain and pour into a serving dish. Toss with
sauce and serve. Be sure to pass the cheese.

4 servings

Spaghetti for the Month of August

SPAGHETTI D'AGOSTO

Eggplant is plentiful—and at its delicious peak—in August, which is when this dish is at its best.

1-pound can Italian peeled plum tomatoes with juice, coarsely chopped

6 fresh basil leaves, chopped

1 whole scallion or spring onion, peeled and diced

1 clove garlic, peeled and crushed

1 medium carrot, peeled and minced

1 stalk or rib of celery, minced

7 tablespoons olive oil

Salt and pepper to taste

1 medium eggplant, peeled and diced

1 pound spaghetti

1 6½-ounce can tuna packed in oil, drained and flaked

1 tablespoon capers, drained and rinsed

10 pitted green olives, halved

In a large saucepan over moderate heat, place tomatoes, basil, scallion, garlic, carrot, and celery. Bring to a boil, lower heat and simmer, covered, for 40 minutes. Remove from heat and carefully pour sauce into the bowl of a food processor fitted with a metal blade. Process for 1 minute. Return the sauce to the saucepan, add 4 tablespoons of olive oil and salt and pepper. Set aside.

In a nonstick sauté pan, heat 3 tablespoons olive oil over moderate heat. Add eggplant, increase heat to high, and cook until the eggplant is golden brown.

In the meantime, cook pasta until al dente. Drain well and transfer to a serving bowl. Toss pasta with tomato sauce, then with eggplant, tuna, capers, and olives. Serve immediately.

4 servings

Rainbow Pasta
PASTA ARCOBALENO

The colorful selection of pasta (the red, white, and green of Italy's
flag) gives this recipe its title. But it's almost as good
using just one color.

2 tablespoons olive oil

1 tablespoon butter

2 scallions or spring onions, bulbs
peeled and minced

3½ ounces Canadian bacon, cut into
matchsticks

5 tablespoons grated Parmesan cheese

1 pound tricolored (spinach, tomato,
white flour) spiral pasta

2 cloves garlic, peeled and minced

½ cup Bechamel Sauce (page 4)

½ cup dry white wine

2 tablespoons minced aromatic herbs
(parsley and basil)

Preheat oven to 400°F.

In a saucepan, heat oil and butter over low heat. When butter has melted,
add scallions and bacon, and sauté until scallions are soft and translucent.
Add bechamel and grated cheese, and cook for 4 minutes.

Cook pasta until al dente, drain, and toss with sauce right in the saucepan.
Pour the entire mixture into an ovenproof dish, sprinkle with aromatic herbs,
and bake for 5 to 10 minutes, or until the top is lightly browned. Remove
from oven and let sit for 5 minutes before serving.

4 servings

Appetizing Bucatini

BUCATINI APPETITOSI

This pasta dish has a magnificent aroma that wafts through the kitchen as the sauce cooks.

2 tablespoons olive oil

12 large green Spanish olives, pitted and sliced in half

1-pound can Italian peeled plum tomatoes, drained and coarsely chopped

5 fresh basil leaves, minced, or 1 teaspoon dried basil

Salt and pepper to taste

½ cup dry white wine

1 pound bucatini, perciatelli or spaghetti

12 ounces sliced boiled ham, diced

3½ ounces mozzarella cheese, diced

3 tablespoons Bechamel Sauce (page 4)

¼ pound butter, sliced into pats

¼ cup grated Parmesan or Pecorino Romano cheese

½ teaspoon fresh or dried oregano

In a large saucepan, heat olive oil over medium heat. Add the olives, tomatoes, and basil. Stir, and season with salt and pepper. Cook for 5 minutes. Add wine and cook for another 5 minutes. Set aside.

Cook the pasta until al dente (about 8 to 10 minutes). Butter an ovenproof dish. Drain pasta, add ham and mozzarella to sauce, and transfer to baking dish. Then toss half of the sauce with the pasta.

Stir bechamel into the remaining sauce, then pour it atop the pasta. Dot with butter, and sprinkle with grated cheese and oregano. Place the pasta under the broiler for 2 minutes. Remove from oven and let it stand for 5 minutes before serving.

4 servings

Anzio

Pasta with Chick-peas and Broccoli

PASTA CON CECI E BROCCOLETTI

This is a thick, delicious one-pot dish, a fact that
makes it one of my favorites.

3 tablespoons olive oil

2 ounces bacon, minced

1 clove garlic, peeled and minced

1 medium head broccoli, broken into
    florets

Salt and pepper to taste

1-pound can chick-peas, drained,
    reserving liquid

1 teaspoon tomato paste

2 chicken bouillon cubes, crumbled and
    dissolved in 2 cups warm water

½ pound fettuccine or any long, flat
    ribbon pasta

2 tablespoons grated Parmesan cheese

In a large saucepan, heat 2 tablespoons olive oil over moderate heat. Add
bacon and garlic, and sauté until bacon begins to crisp. Add broccoli florets
and sauté for 3 minutes. Add the chick-pea liquid and simmer for 1 hour,
adding water, a tablespoon at a time, if the sauce becomes too thick. Season
with salt and pepper.

In a blender, puree 3 tablespoons chick-peas. Add the puree to the broccoli mixture along with the whole chick-peas. Stir in the tomato paste and
chicken broth, and simmer for 10 minutes. Add the uncooked pasta to the
pan, stir gently until pasta begins to soften, then continue cooking until pasta
is al dente.

Pour pasta into a serving bowl, stir in the remaining olive oil, add some
freshly ground black pepper and grated cheese. Toss and serve.

4 servings

This is only a sample of the dishes that feature the bountiful seafood in and around Ostia, the seaport of ancient Rome.

Spaghetti with Garden and Seafood Sauce
SPAGHETTI ORTO MARE

Clams and zucchini combine the light and lovely
tastes of sea and garden.

6 tablespoons olive oil

2 cloves garlic, peeled and crushed

1 cup chopped fresh parsley

2 teaspoons pignoli nuts or shelled walnuts

2 tablespoons grated Parmesan cheese

1 small onion, peeled and chopped

1 scallion, chopped

2 bay leaves

½ chicken bouillon cube, crumbled

4 medium zucchini, diced

1 cup dry white wine

15 ounces minced clams, fresh or canned

5 fresh basil leaves, torn

Salt and pepper to taste

1 pound spaghetti

To make pesto sauce: In the bowl of a food processor fitted with a metal blade, place 2 tablespoons olive oil, 1 garlic clove, ½ cup parsley, pignoli or walnuts, and grated cheese. Process for 2 minutes. Set aside.

To make seafood sauce: In a skillet, heat 2 tablespoons olive oil over moderate heat. Add onion and scallion, and sauté until soft and translucent. Add bay leaves, bouillon cube, and the remainder of the parsley, and cook for 1 minute. Add zucchini and cook for 5 minutes. Stir in ½ cup of wine, and bring to a boil. Boil for 2 minutes, and remove from heat.

In a large skillet, heat 2 tablespoons olive oil over moderate heat. Add minced clams, garlic, and the rest of the wine, and cook for 5 minutes. Add clams to zucchini sauce, stir. Simmer the sauce for 5 minutes, or until slightly reduced. Add basil, and salt and pepper. Remove the sauce from the heat and set aside.

Cook pasta until al dente, drain, and toss with pesto sauce. Pour into a pasta bowl, toss with clam and zucchini sauce, and serve.

4 servings

Herbed Egg Noodles
TAGLIATELLE ALLE ERBE

I hope that fresh herbs are available in your area, for they are what make this dish positively sing!

6 fresh basil leaves, minced

2 tablespoons minced fresh oregano or ¼ teaspoon dried oregano

2 tablespoons minced fresh parsley

3 tablespoons olive oil

½ medium onion, peeled and diced

5 ounces pancetta or bacon, diced

¼ cup unflavored brandy or cognac

3 medium carrots, peeled and julienned

12 ounces flat egg noodles

3 small spring onions or scallions, peeled and chopped

Grated Parmesan or Pecorino Romano cheese

Place minced herbs in a bowl. Stir in 1 tablespoon olive oil and set aside.

In a sauté pan, heat 2 tablespoons olive oil over medium heat. Add onion, spring onions, pancetta, herbs, and brandy, stir, and cook for 2 minutes. Add carrots and cook for another 5 minutes. Remove from heat.

Cook pasta until al dente. Drain quickly and transfer to the sauté pan with the sauce. Heat for 1 minute over medium heat. Serve immediately.

4 servings

Roman-Style Bucatini

BUCATINI ALLA ROMANA

This zesty sauce somehow manages to capture the warm and
sometimes volatile spirit of the Eternal City, where I first
was served this mouthwatering dish.

4 tablespoons olive oil

1 large onion, peeled and diced

1 clove garlic, peeled and minced

2 small hot peppers, minced, or
    1 tablespoon hot pepper flakes

5 ounces pancetta, prosciutto, or bacon,
    cut into matchsticks

½ cup dry red wine

1-pound can Italian peeled plum
    tomatoes, drained and coarsely
    chopped

2 ounces black and green pitted olives,
    cut in half

Salt and pepper to taste

1 pound bucatini or perciatelli

2 ounces grated Pecorino Romano
    cheese

In a large saucepan, heat olive oil over medium flame, add onion, garlic,
and hot peppers, and sauté until onion and garlic are translucent. Add pancetta (or prosciutto or bacon) and brown for about 5 minutes. Stir in wine and
cook until wine evaporates. Add chopped tomatoes, olives, and salt to taste,
and cook sauce until somewhat reduced, about 10 to 15 minutes.

Cook pasta until al dente. Drain quickly and sprinkle with grated cheese.
Toss with sauce, pour into a pasta bowl, and serve very hot.

4 servings

Pescara

Pescara is a gorgeous beach resort whose best dishes are seafood and fish cooked in hundreds of ways.

Pasta with Sole
MAFALDE ALLA SOGLIOLA

A delicate recipe from the memorable Adriatic of Pescara. This dish can be made in a jiffy to satisfy your yen for pasta with the light taste of the sea.

½ teaspoon saffron

½ cup heavy cream

1 cup water

2 fillets of sole (you may use frozen), skinned and cut into 1-inch slices

Salt and pepper to taste

3 tablespoons butter

1 clove garlic, peeled and crushed

1-pound package frozen peas

1 scallion or spring onion, peeled and diced

1 pound mafalde or any long, wide pasta

In a small bowl, dissolve saffron in cream and set aside. In a saucepan, bring water to a boil over high heat. Lower the heat to a simmer, add fish and a dash of salt, cover, and simmer for at least ½ hour. Remove fish with a slotted spoon, reserving the cooking liquid.

In a nonstick skillet, melt 1 tablespoon butter over low heat, add garlic, and sauté until golden. Add fish and cook over very low heat so that fish absorbs the garlic flavor. Do not overcook.

Prepare peas according to package instructions.

In a nonstick skillet, melt 2 tablespoons butter, add scallion and peas, and cook, stirring until vegetables are just heated. Add fish, stirring gently. Pour in fish cooking liquid and saffron-cream mixture. Add salt and pepper, and simmer for 5 minutes.

Cook pasta until al dente. Drain well. Pour into pasta bowl and toss gently with sauce. Serve immediately.

4 servings

Local Wines and Restaurants

Some restaurants where foods typical of the regions can be tasted and regional wines can be sampled:

Region	City	Restaurant
Toscana	Firenze	La Vecchia Cucina Viale de Amicis, 1R

La Vecchia Cucina is a small but pleasing trattoria in the heart of Florence's tourist zone. The atmosphere is friendly and the food is genuinely Tuscan.

Some DOC Wines of Toscana

Tuscany has twenty DOC zones, 90 percent of which produce Chianti.

Bianco di Pitigliano (dry white)

Brunello di Montalcino (dry red)

Chianti Classico (dry red)

Chianti dei Colli Aretini (dry red)

Chianti dei Colli Fiorentini (dry red)

Chianti dei Colli Pisani (dry red)

Chianti dei Colli Senesi (dry red)

Chianti Rufina (dry red)

Galestro (dry white)

Vino Nobile di Montepulciano (dry red)

Vin Santo (sweet white)

Almost all the house wines are very good and inexpensive.

Region	City	Restaurant
Umbria	Assisi	Umbra
		Via degli Archi, 6

Located in the heart of the city near the cathedral and the city hall, Umbra is operated by Alberto Laudenzi. It is a place that offers a delicious Umbrian cuisine, genuine yet adapted to modern tastes and with a concern for modern nutritional values. This restaurant also has a magnificent summer terrace.

Some DOC Wines of Umbria

The most famous white Umbrian wine, even today, is Orvieto, offered in both dry and sweet varieties.

Colli Altotiberini (dry red and whites)

Colli del Trasimeno (dry whites)

Colli Perugini (dry reds, pinks, and whites)

Montefalco (dry red)

Rubesco (dry red)

San Giorgio di Torgiano (dry red)

Solleone (aperitif wine)

Torre di Giano (dry white)

Vin Santo (dessert wine)

Table wines are passable, but nothing to write home about.

Region	City	Restaurant
Marche	Ancona	Passetto
		Piazza IV Novembre

Classic and elegant, Passetto boasts all the comforts you'd expect in an expensive and exclusive restaurant. The huge menu lists many international dishes, but the authentic Marchegiano dishes are easily recognized. Everything prepared here has the mark of impeccable professionalism.

Some DOC Wines of Marche

The most popular Marchegiano wine in both Italy and the United States is Verdicchio.

Bianchello del Metauro (dry white)

Falerio dei Colli Ascolani (dry white)

Rosso Conero (dry red)

Rosso Piceno (dry red)

Verdicchio dei Colli di Jesi (dry white)

Verdicchio di Matélica (dry white)

Vernaccia di Serrapetrona (dry white)

I would pass on the table wines in this region and spend a little extra to savor the DOC wines.

Region	City	Restaurant
Lazio	Roma	Cannavota
		Piazza San Giovanni in Laterano

Cannavota is a typical friendly trattoria, sometimes noisy but Roman to the nth degree. It is directly opposite the Basilica of St. John in Lateran. The owner, Dante Furnari, is nicknamed "Cannavota" because he is as tall and thin as a cane of straw. The kitchen is good, the portions generous, the service fast and courteous, and the prices are moderate. Try the Pasta all' Arrabbiata, a spicy, hot pasta dressed with tomato sauce, pungent with garlic and red hot peppers—unforgettable.

Some DOC Wines of Lazio

Lazio is the region of central Italy that produces world-famous white wines:

Est!-Est!!-Est!!! di Montefiascone (dry white)
Frascati (dry white)

Some Lazio reds are also very good:

Aleatico di Gradoli (red, sweet dessert wine)
Cerveteri (dry white and red)
Merlot (dry red)
Sangiovese (dry red)

Good table wines include:

Colle Picchioni dei Castelli
Castelli Romani
Torre Ercolana di Anagni

Region	City	Restaurant
Abruzzi	Aquila	Scannapapera Località Pile

To reach Scannapapera take the highway toward Rome, and exit at Pile. Very soon, you will see a sign indicating the way to this unexpected place of culinary surprises inspired by the truest Abruzzese traditions. The restaurant is comfortable and easygoing, the owner and his wife make you feel right at home, and the food is wholesome and delicious.

The DOC Wines of Abruzzi

Montepulciano Cerasuolo d'Abruzzo (dry red)

Montepulciano d'Abruzzo (dry red)

Trebbiano d'Abruzzo (dry white)

Some good table wines include:

Moscato Bianco (sweet white)

Rustico dell' Alta Val Peligna (red)

Spinello (dry white)

Chapter 3

The Sumptuous Pastas of Southern Italy

Introducing the Region

A land where tomatoes ripen in the clear, sparkling sunshine, where the ancient Greek civilization flourished, where nature has asserted itself with the fury of volcanoes—this is the southern Italy that awaits you. Immersed in earthy essences, in the strange light between magic and reality, you will discover an enchanted place carved from earth and granite. Both its strong and harsh aspects induce those who speak of southern Italy to do so with an awed passion. There is the eternal movement of Italy's blue-green sea offering up its denizens for myriad delicious dishes; jagged cliffs; velvety sands; fragrant orange trees and jasmine; and of course the haughty olive trees—providing their superb fruit and oil. The silver foliage of these trees recalls generations of grandparents who still know the stories of olden times and ancient truths.

Molise is a region of mountain villages, quaint customs, and truly unforgettable cuisine—natural, light, and uncomplicated. Farming and sheepherding are the principal occupations of this hilly terrain.

Puglia's capital is Bari, a bustling city noted for olive oil, wine, and pasta. Some other places I've enjoyed visiting in my travels include Lecce, the site of gorgeous Baroque architecture, and Altamura, whose bread is prized throughout Italy. The attraction in Alberobello is the unique *trulli*, conical stone homes built without the use of mortar. Tourists also head for Gargano, a peninsula in the Adriatic Sea that has white sand beaches, clear water, good hotels, and, for those of us who always appreciate a good meal, some fine restaurants.

San Giovanni Rotondo is the town where the Franciscan monastery of the same name attracts thousands of pilgrims who come to see the residence of the most famous stigmatist of our time, Padre Pio. Not too far away is Gallipoli, a lovely beach resort on the Adriatic whose white sand and clear warm water remind one of the Caribbean Islands. But this is Italy, no doubt about it, because a few paces from the beach are rows of restaurants, and from them waft the delicious aromas of local cooking.

Campania, where the cuisine is as lively and varied as its population, is the home of San Marzano tomatoes, absolutely the best plum tomatoes in the world. It is also the area where Mount Vesuvius erupted in A.D. 90, destroying Herculaneum (Ercolano) and Pompei. And of course there's Naples, a great sprawl of noise and confusion with a cuisine all its own. The fare here is wonderfully varied, reflective of the foreign invasions that Naples has endured over the centuries. (If you didn't know that Naples was once dominated by Arab cultures, you would wonder why many Neapolitans add pine nuts and sweet raisins to their meatballs.)

Basilicata shares its northern border with Campania, and the regional dialect and cuisine are heavily Neapolitan. Its southern border touches Calabria, so the dialect and cuisine in this southern area are more Calabrian than Neapolitan.

Calabria, the last of five regions in the southern peninsula, is divided into three provinces: Cosenza, Catanzaro, and Reggio Calabria. This is the region I know best because my parents were born there. (I will have much more to say about Calabria later on.)

One of the most appealing places in Calabria is Bagnara, a small fishing village on the Tyrrhenian coast in the province of Reggio Calabria. Here, houses cling to the hillside, and as you climb the narrow streets, you can smell the tantalizing aroma of freshly baked whole wheat bread. The women of the town, dressed in traditional long skirts and beautiful linen head shawls, run the whole show. The men (except the very old) are nowhere to be seen: They are fishermen, and hunt the surrounding sea for swordfish. Truly, to visit Bagnara is to journey into the past.

Another area that echoes its past is Cosenza, Calabria's northern province, which is home to thousands of Albanian immigrants, who have retained their customs, language, and religion. Ancient history is also reflected in Bova, a little town on the Ionian coast whose residents speak Italian, Calabrian (a mixture of Italian, Spanish, and Greek), and Grecanico (an Italianization of classical Greek).

Sicilia is a semiautonomous, almost independent, region of Italy. Its language is unique because it is a confluence of the languages of the many peoples who invaded and colonized the island through the centuries: Arabs, Swabians (Germans), Bourbons, Spanish and, finally, Italians. Like its language, the food of Sicily has been influenced by the varied cuisines of those cultures.

Sicilia has many interesting towns, villages and cities, on and off the beaten path. During my visits to this historic island, I've seen some fascinating places: Enna, at the very center of the region, was the refuge of Sicilia's original tribes, the Sicul, when their island was first invaded. Here traces of the most primitive Sicilian civilization can be found. Taormina, a city of fantastic views and delicious marzipan, is nestled in the hills that surround Mount Etna, Europe's most active volcano. This city was Winston Churchill's favorite vacation retreat and, after Stresa on Lago Maggiore, it is mine.

Other places I've enjoyed visiting include Agrigento, the site of the largest

Greek temples in the world, and Siracusa, once the most powerful city in Magna Grecia, where there are more ruins of Greek temples than in Greece itself! In the extreme southern part of Sicilia is Ragusa, where the dialect, architecture, and cuisine are strongly Arabic. The town of Corleone—made famous by Mario Puzo's extraordinary novel *The Godfather*—is a charming mountain village, but when I visited it, I kept getting unnerving mental flashbacks of the movie trilogy inspired by the novel. Not to worry, however; the people are open and gracious once they know you are "Mericano," American.

Sardegna is the last of the twenty regions of Italy that we'll visit in this section of the book. On this enchanting island, one can still find fortresslike buildings (*nuraghi*) that remain from prehistoric times. The Sardinian coasts are magnificent, the plains intensely cultivated, and the hills provide pastures for innumerable sheep and goats. The mountainous interior is covered with deep forests where brigands still rule with the *lupara,* a sawed-off shotgun that was once used to kill wolves. The regional language is a mixture of Spanish (Catalán), French, and Italian, and the superb cuisine, which uses the varied local meat and produce, is simple yet rich.

One of the most intriguing places I've stopped in is Nuoro, a small village in the center of Sardegna where time has stood still. Here the people dress in costumes of the Middle Ages, and isolation preserves their customs. A visit to Nuoro is a visit to a time when life was simple and uncomplicated, as is the cuisine of this special little village.

Now, as you taste the marvelous dishes of the South, I wish you *cent'anni!*—a hundred years of healthy and happy life!

Perciatelli with Smoked Meat Sauce

PERCIATELLI AFFUMICATI

In the old days, before refrigeration, meats were preserved by smoking. The flavor of smoked meats is so fantastic that the practice has persisted. This dish is a hearty reminder of simpler times.

1 medium onion, peeled and thinly sliced

3 ounces smoked bacon, preferably Canadian

2 tablespoons butter

1-pound can Italian peeled plum tomatoes, drained and coarsely chopped

1 small hot pepper, minced, or ½ teaspoon hot pepper flakes

Salt to taste

1 pound perciatelli or bucatini

¼ cup grated Parmesan or Pecorino Romano cheese

In a large saucepan, sauté onion and bacon in butter over low heat until bacon is lightly browned and onion is soft and translucent. Stir often with a wooden spoon. Stir in tomatoes, hot pepper, and a dash of salt. Adjust heat to medium, cover, and cook for 10 minutes.

Cook pasta until al dente, drain quickly, and transfer to the saucepan. Stir gently and cook 1 more minute. Toss with grated cheese and transfer to a serving dish.

4 servings

Great Taste Pasta

FUSILLI GRAN SAPORE

The rich combination of cheeses and eggplant supplies the "great taste." When visiting friends in Isernia I devoured one plateful and, to the delight of my hosts, I asked for more, it was that good.

8 tablespoons olive oil (preferably extra-virgin)

1 large clove garlic, peeled and crushed

2 1-pound cans Italian peeled plum tomatoes, drained and very coarsely chopped

10 fresh basil leaves or 1 teaspoon dried basil

Salt to taste

4 small eggplants, peeled and cubed

½ pound mozzarella cheese, cubed

1 pound fusilli or other corkscrew pasta

¼ cup grated Pecorino Romano or Parmesan cheese

Heat 4 tablespoons oil in a large saucepan over low heat. Add garlic, and sauté until golden. Add tomatoes, basil, and salt. Cover and cook, stirring often, for 30 minutes.

In a skillet, heat 4 tablespoons olive oil. Add eggplant and fry until cubes are lightly browned. Remove eggplant from skillet and place on absorbent paper towels to drain. Transfer eggplant to a serving bowl, stir in mozzarella.

Cook pasta until al dente. Drain well. Toss with eggplant and mozzarella. Finally, pour tomato sauce over the pasta, toss gently, sprinkle with grated cheese, and serve.

4 servings

Penne with Very Sharp Provolone Cheese

PENNE CON CACIO PICCANTI

A zingy pasta dish that often requires more than one glass of wine to cool the flames!

2 pounds broccoli florets

4 tablespoons olive oil

2 ounces pancetta, prosciutto, or boiled ham, julienned

1 hot jalapeño pepper, diced, or 1 tablespoon hot pepper flakes

1 clove garlic, peeled and crushed

2 tablespoons dry white wine

1 pound penne or rigatoni

3 tablespoons grated very sharp provolone cheese

Boil broccoli florets in salted water for 10 minutes. Drain well and set aside.

In a large, deep skillet, heat olive oil over moderate heat. Add pancetta, jalapeño, and garlic. Cook for 5 minutes. Adjust heat to high and add broccoli, sauté for 2 minutes, then stir in wine. Cook for 2 more minutes and set aside.

Cook pasta until al dente. Drain well. Transfer to a bowl and toss with broccoli sauce. Sprinkle with grated cheese and serve immediately.

4 servings

Penne Pasta, Peasant Style

PENNE DEL CONTADINO

This delicious pasta was designed to restore the strength of hardworking peasants.

1 large eggplant, peeled and cubed

½ cup vegetable oil (for frying eggplant)

1 tablespoon butter

2 tablespoons olive oil

2 medium onions, peeled and diced

1-pound can Italian peeled plum tomatoes, drained and chopped

Salt and pepper to taste

1 6½-ounce can tuna packed in oil, drained and flaked

3 ounces pitted black olives, halved

8 fresh basil leaves, torn, or 1 teaspoon dried basil

¼ teaspoon dried thyme

1 pound penne or rigatoni

1 tablespoon grated Parmesan cheese

1 pound mozzarella cheese, cubed

In a large skillet, fry eggplant in vegetable oil until light brown. Remove eggplant with a slotted spoon and transfer to paper towels to drain.

In a large saucepan, melt butter and olive oil over moderate heat. Add onions and sauté until lightly browned. Add tomatoes, season with salt and pepper, stir, and cook for 20 minutes, uncovered. Add eggplant, flaked tuna, black olives, basil, and thyme to sauce and cook for 10 more minutes. Remove from heat and set aside.

Cook pasta until al dente. Drain well. Pour into a serving bowl, toss with sauce, sprinkle with grated cheese and mozzarella cubes.

4 servings

Taranto

Legend has it that the tarantella, a popular Italian folk dance, traces its origins to Taranto. As the tale goes, when someone was bitten by a tarantula, he or she had to dance the tarantella to overcome the effects of the venom.

Most Flavorful Egg Noodles
TAGLIATELLE SAPORITISSIME

The blend of tender squid with earthy wild mushrooms makes for a particularly tasty pasta.

4 tablespoons olive oil

2 cloves garlic, peeled and crushed

¼ cup chopped fresh parsley

2 small fresh squid, cleaned and sliced into rings (or use frozen squid)

½ cup dry white wine

1 ounce dried porcini mushrooms, (or other strong flavored mushrooms), rehydrated in 1 cup cold water for ½ hour, then chopped

Salt and pepper

16 ounces canned tomato sauce

1 small hot pepper or 1 teaspoon hot pepper flakes

1 pound long, flat egg noodles

In a large saucepan, heat olive oil over moderate heat. Add garlic and parsley, and sauté for 2 minutes. Adjust heat to high, add squid rings, and cook until they release their liquid, at least 2 to 3 minutes. Stir in wine and cook for a minute or so until wine evaporates. Add mushrooms, and lower heat to medium. Stir sauce with a wooden spoon and cook for 2 minutes. Add salt and pepper, tomato sauce, and hot pepper, and stir and simmer for 20 minutes.

Cook pasta until al dente. Drain well. Pour into a bowl, toss with sauce, and serve.

4 servings

Brindisi
Two-Flavored Linguine
LINGUINE DUE SAPORI

I discovered this marvelous dish in Brindisi, the seaside town where the ferry leaves for Greece. The delicate shrimp and the pungent arugula work especially well together.

½ pound small shrimp, fresh or frozen

½ cup water

1 cup dry white wine

2 fresh basil leaves

Salt and pepper to taste

2 tablespoons olive oil

1 tablespoon unsalted butter

2 small leeks, washed carefully and thinly sliced

2 cloves garlic, peeled and minced

1 small bunch arugula

5 ounces ricotta cheese

2 tablespoons grated Parmesan cheese

¼ cup heavy cream

1 pound linguine

If you're using frozen shrimp, defrost first. Bring water, wine, basil leaves, a dash of salt, and a sprinkle of pepper to a boil in a saucepan. Toss in the shrimp and cook for 2 minutes. Drain shrimp in a colander and set aside, reserving the pasta water. Place oil and butter in a saucepan over medium heat, add 1 sliced leek and ½ the minced garlic. Sauté until soft.

Add cooked shrimp to saucepan, along with salt and pepper, and the reserved pasta water. Lower the heat to a simmer.

Place the arugula, ricotta, remaining minced garlic, grated cheese, and cream in the bowl of a food processor fitted with the metal blade.

Process until almost homogenized, about 1 minute. Correct seasoning and pour over cooked shrimp sauce. Stir and allow the sauce to simmer for 3 minutes. Cover and turn off heat.

Cook pasta until al dente, drain, and add to the sauce. Toss and serve immediately.

4 servings

Fusilli, Garden Style

FUSILLI DELL'ORTO

The best time to prepare this recipe is when the freshest vegetables and herbs are in season. If the weather is right, this is the perfect dish for dining al fresco.

½ pound fresh green beans

3 cups water

3 tablespoons olive oil

2 cloves garlic, peeled and minced

1 pound fusilli or corkscrew pasta

1 yellow bell pepper, roasted, peeled, and cut into strips

10 fresh basil leaves, chopped

Salt and pepper to taste

¼ cup grated Pecorino Romano or Parmesan cheese

Wash beans, snip off each end, and halve. In a saucepan, bring lightly salted water to a boil. Immerse beans, and cook for 15 to 20 minutes. When done, drain in a colander, reserving 1½ cups pasta water.

In a nonstick skillet, heat olive oil over medium heat. Add garlic and sauté for 3 minutes. Add green beans, stir, and cook for another minute.

Cook pasta until al dente, then drain well. Pour pasta into a serving bowl. Add bean mixture, bell pepper strips, basil leaves, reserved pasta water, black pepper and, finally, the grated cheese. Toss and serve.

4 servings

Pasta Pie with Truffles

TIMBALLO AL TARTUFO

When I was served this spectacular, aromatic dish in Lecce, I couldn't
decide whether to photograph it or simply dig in.
My appetite won out.

I tablespoon butter

I medium onion, peeled and diced

8 ounces boiled ham, diced

½ cup dry white wine

Salt and pepper to taste

Dash nutmeg

8 ounces ricotta cheese

I small (I ounce) tube of white truffle
paste (optional)

½ cup Bechamel Sauce (page 4)

¼ cup grated Parmesan cheese

2 large egg yolks (save whites to brush
on crust)

12 ounces tricolored corkscrew pasta

I pound frozen pie dough, defrosted

In a large saucepan, melt butter over medium heat. Add onion and ham,
and sauté until onion is translucent. Add wine, salt and pepper, and nutmeg,
and cook for 10 minutes.

In a bowl, beat together ricotta, truffle paste, if desired, ¼ cup bechamel,
2 tablespoons grated Parmesan, and egg yolks. Add this mixture to the saucepan, stir, and remove from heat.

Cook pasta until *very* al dente. Drain quickly and add to sauce. Toss well.

Preheat oven to 400°F.

Stretch defrosted pie dough into a deep ovenproof dish, push dough down
to fit dish, leaving enough dough hanging over the sides of the dish.

Fill the crust with the pasta and sauce, sprinkle with the remaining grated
cheese, and cover with bechamel. Fold over the hanging dough into dish.
Beat the egg whites until frothy and brush onto pie crust. Bake the pie for
20 to 25 minutes until browned. Remove from the oven and allow to cool for
5 minutes before serving.

4 servings

The Miller's Wife's Pasta

FUSILLI ALLA MUGNAIA

The original recipe called for the miller's wife to make pasta from her
husband's freshly ground flour, but storebought will certainly do.
A thick and rich dish, redolent of veal and mushrooms.

2 tablespoons butter

2 tablespoons olive oil

1¼ pounds (20 ounces) ground veal

1 large onion, peeled and sliced

½ stalk celery, diced

Salt and pepper to taste

½ cup dry white wine

4 canned Italian plum tomatoes,
  drained and coarsely chopped

2 ounces dried porcini mushrooms or
  other good variety of mushroom,
  soaked for ½ hour in water,
  drained through a fine mesh
  strainer (reserving liquid), and
  chopped

1 cup beef stock

1 scant tablespoon all-purpose flour

1 pound fusilli (spaghetti will work here
  as well)

¼ cup grated Pecorino Romano or
  Parmesan cheese

In a large saucepan over low heat, melt butter and olive oil. Raise heat
to medium, add veal, onion, and celery. Season with salt and pepper, and
cook until well browned, stirring often, about 15 minutes. Add wine and cook
for another 15 minutes.

Add tomatoes, mushrooms, and mushroom liquid, and cook for 15
minutes. Add beef stock and cook, uncovered, for another 15 minutes.

Whisk in flour and cook for 10 minutes more. Cook pasta until al dente,
drain well, and pour into saucepan. Toss and transfer into serving bowl.
Sprinkle with grated cheese and serve very hot.

4 servings

Pasta with Zucchini and Tomatoes

PASTA ZUCCHINE E POMODORI

Here's a deliciously soupy version of pasta with summer vegetables.

1 tablespoon butter

1 tablespoon olive oil

1 clove garlic, peeled and crushed

1 pound medium zucchini, julienned

½-pound can Italian peeled plum
   tomatoes, drained and chopped

1 quart hot water

2 chicken bouillon cubes

½ pound spaghetti or thin spaghetti

½ cup chopped fresh basil

Black pepper to taste

Grated Parmesan cheese

In a large saucepan, melt butter and olive oil over moderate heat. Add garlic and zucchini, and sauté until zucchini is light brown. Add tomatoes and cook for 5 minutes, then add hot water and bouillon cubes. Bring to a boil and add uncooked pasta, cook until pasta is al dente, about 10 to 12 minutes.

When pasta is ready, add basil, stir, and pour into a serving bowl. Sprinkle with black pepper and serve. Pass the grated cheese.

4 servings

Ercolano (Herculaneum)

Aphrodite's Linguine
LINGUINE AFRODITE

There is a legend that wives can quickly invigorate their weary husbands by preparing this pasta dish. Even if it doesn't work as an aphrodisiac, you'll still have made a wonderful meal.

1-pound can crushed Italian plum tomatoes

1 clove garlic, peeled and crushed

1 celery heart, sliced thinly

5 tablespoons olive oil

Salt and pepper to taste

1 pound linguine or spaghetti

2 small carrots, thinly sliced

In a saucepan, bring tomatoes and garlic to a boil, and add celery and 4 tablespoons olive oil. Stir vigorously, add salt and pepper, and simmer, uncovered, for 20 minutes.

Cook pasta until al dente. Drain well and pour into a serving bowl. Toss with sauce, carrots, and the remaining olive oil. Let stand, covered, for 5 minutes before serving.

4 servings

Tricolored Bucatini

BUCATINI TRICOLORI

This is a marvelously spicy meal. If you want to adjust the flavor (from lukewarm to fiery and vice versa), reduce or increase the amount of jalapeño pepper accordingly.

4 tablespoons olive oil

I clove garlic, peeled and crushed

I jalapeño pepper, minced, or
 I tablespoon hot pepper flakes

I medium eggplant, peeled and diced

2 cups Basic Tomato Sauce (page 3)

I small yellow bell pepper, seeded and
 julienned

2 ounces black and green pitted olives,
 halved

I tablespoon capers, rinsed and drained

I pound bucatini or perciatelli

¼ cup chopped fresh parsley

Heat olive oil in a large saucepan over low heat. Add garlic and jalapeño, and cook until garlic is golden, being careful not to brown. Add eggplant and cook over low heat until eggplant is soft and translucent. Add tomato sauce, bell pepper strips, olives, and capers, stir, and cover.

Let sauce simmer for 10 minutes. In the meantime, cook pasta until al dente, then drain well. Toss pasta with sauce and simmer together for 2 minutes. Pour into a pasta bowl, sprinkle with parsley, and serve.

4 servings

Neapolitan Egg Noodles

TAGLIATELLE NAPOLETANE

This meal is so authentically Neapolitan that you may find yourself breaking into Naples's quintessential song "O Sole Mio."

4 tablespoons olive oil

½ large onion, peeled and diced

¼ pound boiled ham, diced

1-pound can Italian peeled plum tomatoes, drained and chopped

Salt and pepper to taste

2 small eggplants, unpeeled and cubed

2 bell peppers, 1 yellow, 1 red, seeded and julienned

1 pound long, flat egg noodles

½ cup grated sharp Pecorino Romano cheese

5 fresh basil leaves

In a large saucepan, heat olive oil over medium heat. Add onion and sauté until it is translucent. Add ham, stir, and cook for 3 minutes. Add tomatoes, salt and pepper, and simmer, covered, for 30 minutes.

Fry eggplant cubes and bell pepper strips in deep fryer until golden brown. Remove with a slotted spoon and drain on paper towels.

Cook pasta until al dente. Drain well and pour into a serving bowl. Toss with the tomato sauce, fried eggplant, bell peppers, and grated cheese. Add basil, toss again, and serve. Pass more grated cheese.

4 servings

Rigatoni with Shrimp Sauce

RIGATONI AI GAMBERI

Although Capri is the most famous island in the Bay of Naples, I think Ischia is more enchanting. It's a lovely island of fishing villages where authentic Neapolitan pasta and seafood abound. This recipe always makes me think of that magical isle.

5 tablespoons olive oil

2 cloves garlic, peeled and crushed

½ pound mushrooms, sliced

Salt and pepper

½ cup dry white wine

¼ cup chopped fresh parsley

6 canned Italian plum tomatoes, drained and chopped

16 large shrimp, peeled, deveined, and diced

1 pound rigatoni

1 small package saffron

In a saucepan, heat 3 tablespoons olive oil over moderate heat. Add one crushed garlic clove and sauté until golden. Add mushrooms and cook over high heat for 10 minutes. Add salt and pepper to taste. Add wine and cook until wine evaporates, about 5 minutes. Stir in parsley and remove the saucepan from the heat.

In another saucepan, heat 2 tablespoons olive oil over moderate heat. Add remaining crushed garlic clove and sauté until golden. Add tomatoes and cook over high heat for 10 minutes. Add shrimp to tomato sauce and cook, stirring, over moderate heat for 4 minutes. Remove from heat but cover to keep warm.

Cook pasta until al dente, adding saffron to cooking water. Drain well and toss with mushroom sauce. Pour into a serving dish and toss with shrimp and tomato sauce. Garnish with more chopped parsley and serve.

4 servings

Picturesquely situated on a peaceful peninsula in the Bay of Naples, Sorrento is famous for its seafood.

Linguine with Large Shrimp
LINGUINE CON I GAMBERI

In this delightful dish, the taste of the sea is provided by fresh Mediterranean prawns, which look a bit like small lobsters. However, jumbo shrimp work just as well.

6 tablespoons olive oil

1 small onion, peeled and diced

4 cloves garlic, peeled and crushed

2 bell peppers, 1 red, 1 yellow, seeded and diced

1-pound can Italian peeled plum tomatoes

5 fresh basil leaves, chopped

Salt and pepper

1 teaspoon sugar

2 cloves garlic, sliced

8 prawns or jumbo shrimp, shelled and deveined

1 pound linguine

Heat 3 tablespoons olive oil in a skillet. Add onion and crushed garlic, and sauté until onion is translucent. Add bell peppers, tomatoes, basil, salt and pepper to taste, and sugar. Stir, lower heat to simmer and cook, uncovered, for 15 minutes.

Put sliced garlic into a bowl along with 3 tablespoons olive oil and salt and pepper to taste. Add shrimp, cover the bowl, and marinate the shrimp for 20 minutes.

Cook pasta until al dente. While pasta is cooking, remove shrimp from marinade. Cook shrimp on grill or broil 4 minutes each side. Drain pasta well. Pour into a serving bowl, toss with sauce, and place shrimp on top. (Don't be greedy—only two shrimp to a person!)

4 servings

Shell Pasta, Hometown Style

CONCHIGLIE PAESANE

A jewel of a town, Amalfi is rich in history and culture. The hills surrounding it are intensely cultivated, and this recipe features a satisfying blend of local produce and shell pasta, shaped to catch every delicious drop of the light sauce.

4 tablespoons olive oil

I large onion, peeled and diced

I large clove garlic, peeled and crushed

I large carrot, peeled and diced

I stalk celery, diced

¼ pound sliced boiled ham, diced

I-pound can Italian peeled plum tomatoes, drained and chopped

I bay leaf

Salt and pepper

I-pound can chick-peas, (ceci or garbanzos), drained

I pound medium pasta shells

¼ cup chopped fresh parsley

¼ cup grated Parmesan cheese

Heat oil in a large saucepan over medium heat. Add onion, garlic, carrot, and celery, and cook until onion is golden. Add ham, cook for 5 minutes, then add tomatoes and bay leaf. Add salt and pepper to taste, cover, and cook for 10 minutes. Add chick-peas, cover, and simmer for 20 minutes.

Cook pasta until al dente, drain well, add to saucepan, stir, and simmer for 5 minutes.

Pour pasta and sauce into a serving bowl, sprinkle with fresh parsley and grated cheese, toss, and serve.

4 servings

Vegetarian Spaghetti

SPAGHETTI VEGETARIANI

Although Capri is a must-see, it is a bit overrun for my taste.
However, I had this dish in a tiny Caprese mom-and-pop restaurant off
the beaten track. I don't know if I could find the place again, but
the owners graciously gave me this recipe.

3 tablespoons olive oil

1 large onion, peeled and chopped

5 medium zucchini, diced

2 large Savoy cabbage leaves, cut into
very thin strips

4 large romaine lettuce leaves, cut into
thin strips

½ large red bell pepper, diced

Salt and pepper

1 pound spaghetti

2 large eggs

¼ cup grated Parmesan cheese

Dash nutmeg

In a large skillet, heat olive oil over medium heat. Add onion and sauté
until soft and lightly browned. Add zucchini, cabbage, lettuce, bell pepper,
and salt and pepper to taste, cover, and simmer 15 to 20 minutes.

In the meantime, cook pasta until al dente. While pasta is cooking, beat
the eggs with a dash of salt and grated cheese in a serving bowl. Drain pasta,
saving ¼ cup pasta water, and add to egg mixture. Add cooked vegetables
and dash of nutmeg, toss well, add the pasta water and toss again. Serve
pasta, and pass the grated cheese.

4 servings

Adalgisa's Spaghetti
SPAGHETTI DELL'ADALGISA

Perhaps this dish was named for a queen of Naples, Adalgisa, who is said to have led a rather spicy life. But the dish is so scrumptious that you don't need a legend to fall in love with it.

½ cup vegetable oil (for frying eggplant)

I medium eggplant, peeled and cubed, and processed as described on page 2

5 tablespoons olive oil

I clove garlic, peeled and crushed

I-pound can Italian peeled plum tomatoes, drained and chopped

Salt and pepper to taste

I cup fresh basil leaves, chopped, or I teaspoon dried basil

I pound spaghetti

Romano cheese

Heat vegetable oil in a deep skillet until very hot. Add eggplant and fry until it is golden brown. Remove with a slotted spoon and place on paper towels to drain.

Heat olive oil in a large saucepan over moderate heat. Add garlic and sauté for 1 minute. Add tomatoes, season with salt and pepper, and cook for 10 minutes over high heat, stirring constantly. Remove pan from heat, add basil, and stir.

Cook pasta until al dente. Drain and pour into a serving bowl. Toss the pasta with grated cheese, then toss with the sauce. Finally, add eggplant and toss lightly. Serve.

4 servings

Acquafredda di Maratea

Spaghetti, Maratea Style

SPAGHETTI ALLA MARATEA

If you enjoy seafood sauce over pasta, this simple recipe will surely fill the bill. Even if you live miles from the ocean, the ingredients are readily available in most supermarkets.

4 tablespoons olive oil

4 small fillets canned anchovies, rinsed and minced

2 large onions, peeled and thinly sliced

½ cup chicken broth

Salt and pepper to taste

1 6½-ounce can tuna fish packed in oil, drained and flaked

2 tablespoons heavy cream

1 pound spaghetti

½ cup chopped fresh parsley

In a large skillet, heat oil over moderate heat. Add anchovies and onions. As soon as onions begin to soften, slowly begin to add the broth and cook until the broth is reduced, about 5 minutes. Season with salt and pepper.

Add flaked tuna and cream, stir, and cook for 5 more minutes. Remove from the heat and set aside.

Cook pasta until al dente. Drain well and pour into the skillet with the sauce, stir, and heat for 2 minutes over high heat. Transfer to a serving bowl, sprinkle with chopped parsley, and serve.

4 servings

Seafood Spaghetti

SPAGHETTI MARINARA

This seafood specialty with an Italian name is a familiar
one for American pasta fans.

4 tablespoons olive oil

1 small onion, peeled and diced

1 clove garlic, peeled and crushed

9 ounces frozen shrimp, defrosted

9 ounces canned mussels, drained and
    left whole

9 ounces canned minced clams, drained

1/2 cup dry white wine

Salt and pepper to taste

Pinch dried thyme

Pinch dried marjoram

1 cup canned or fresh tomato sauce

1/4 cup chopped fresh parsley

1 pound spaghetti

In a large saucepan, heat olive oil over moderate heat. Add onion and
garlic, and sauté until onion is translucent. Add shrimp, mussels, clams,
and wine, and cook until wine evaporates. Add salt and pepper and herbs,
and cook for 3 minutes. Add tomato sauce, stir, and simmer for 10 minutes.
Remove from heat, add chopped parsley, and stir.

Cook pasta until al dente. Drain well. Pour into a serving bowl, toss with
sauce, and serve.

4 servings

Potenza

The capital of the almost-forgotten region of Basilicata is Potenza. The city is very old and sparsely populated, but the food is unforgettable.

Bow-Tie Macaroni in Rich Sauce
FARFALLE ALLA RICCA

I first enjoyed this dish in a small restaurant, and it was indeed as rich and filling as its name suggests. In fact, while it meant the farfalle were as a first course, I was so satisfied that I settled for a cup of strong espresso as my main course.

4 tablespoons olive oil

1 clove garlic, peeled and minced

11 ounces fresh turkey breast, sliced into thin strips

1 14-ounce can Italian peeled plum tomatoes, drained and chopped

6 fresh basil leaves, minced

Salt and pepper to taste

12 ounces bow-tie pasta

12 pitted black olives, halved

2 ounces sharp provolone cheese, shaved or thinly sliced

Heat olive oil in a large skillet. Add garlic and sauté until golden. Stir in the turkey and cook until the meat is light brown. Stir in tomatoes, basil, and a dash of salt and pepper. Simmer, uncovered, for 20 minutes.

Cook pasta until al dente. Drain pasta and add to turkey sauce along with olives. Stir and cook for 2 minutes.

Sprinkle provolone cheese shavings on pasta, add black pepper to taste, and stir gently until cheese melts. Serve hot.

4 servings

Bagnara

Pasta with Chick-peas and Clams

PASTA E CECI CON LE VONGOLE

This is a spectacular version of Italian clam chowder that's traditionally served during the wintertime.

5 tablespoons olive oil

1 clove garlic, peeled and crushed

½ cup chopped fresh parsley

1 teaspoon dried rosemary, crushed into a powder

1 tablespoon hot pepper flakes

2 canned Italian peeled plum tomatoes, drained and chopped

1 quart water

2 chicken bouillon cubes

1 pound ditalini or any short tubular pasta

1-pound can chick-peas, drained

1-pound can minced clams

Pepper to taste

In a large saucepan, heat olive oil over moderate heat. Add garlic, rosemary, hot pepper flakes, and ½ of parsley. Sauté for 3 minutes. Add tomatoes, water, bouillon cubes, and bring to a boil. Add uncooked pasta and chick-peas.

When pasta is al dente, add clams, clam juice, and the remaining chopped parsley. Add black pepper, stir, and cook for another minute or two. Pour into a serving bowl and serve.

4 servings

An ancient and beautiful city, Catanzaro, is the capital of Calabria.

Delicious Linguine

LINGUINE DELIZIOSE

White vinegar brings out the bright colors and flavors of the vegetables in this luscious sauce. I tried preparing this dish without vinegar, and found it wanting—the acid adds the needed zing.

4 tablespoons olive oil

½ eggplant, peeled and diced

I large zucchini, diced

Salt and pepper to taste

I tablespoon minced fresh parsley

8 ounces porcini, portobello, shiitake, or any strong-tasting mushroom

I large garlic clove, peeled and minced

½ teaspoon dried marjoram

I tablespoon white vinegar

I pound linguine

Grated Parmesan cheese

In a large saucepan, heat olive oil until it is almost smoking. Add eggplant, zucchini, and salt and pepper. Lower heat to medium and cook, uncovered, for 15 minutes. Remove vegetables with a slotted spoon, draining off as much of the oil as possible. Place on a plate, sprinkle with parsley, and cover to keep the vegetables warm.

In the same pan, add mushrooms and garlic to leftover oil and sauté for 5 minutes. Add the zucchini and eggplant, sprinkle with marjoram, salt to taste, and vinegar.

Cook pasta until al dente, drain quickly, and toss pasta into the sauce. Top with grated cheese and serve immediately.

4 servings

Small Ribbon Pasta with Fava or Lima Beans

TAGLIATELLE CON LE FAVE

I was served this dish in a small Albanian village, where I raved
so much about it that my kind hostess finally,
if reluctantly, gave me the recipe.

1 large onion, peeled and minced

1 tablespoon olive oil

2 slices of pancetta, prosciutto, or
   boiled ham, minced

1 pound fresh or frozen fava or
   lima beans

1¼ cups canned tomato sauce

1 fresh jalapeño pepper or 1 teaspoon
   hot pepper flakes

Salt

1 pound flat egg noodles

1 tablespoon minced parsley

1 teaspoon minced chervil (optional)

Grated Parmesan cheese

In a large skillet, sauté onion in olive oil until soft and translucent. Add pancetta and cook for 1 minute. Add beans and simmer over low heat for 5 minutes.

Add tomato sauce, jalapeño pepper, and dash of salt. Stir, cover, and simmer for 20 minutes.

In the meantime, cook noodles until al dente. Drain, saving ¼ cup pasta water. Pour pasta in a heated serving bowl, add pasta water, toss with the bean sauce, sprinkle with parsley and chervil, if desired, and serve. Pass the grated cheese.

4 servings

Spicy Bucatini

BUCATINI PICANTI

The spiciness of this dish comes from the natural heat of the peppers and the sharp flavor of the cheese. You can adjust these ingredients if you want to raise or lower the temperature of this zingy pasta. (If you wish to make this dish richer, double the amount of meat.)

1 tablespoon butter

2 tablespoons olive oil

1 large onion, peeled and diced

2 jalapeño or cayenne peppers, diced, or 1 tablespoon hot pepper flakes

1½ ounces bacon, diced

3½ ounces fatback, diced

1-pound can Italian peeled plum tomatoes, drained and chopped

1 pound bucatini or perciatelli (you can also use spaghetti)

2 ounces very sharp Pecorino Romano cheese, grated

Heat butter and olive oil in a large saucepan over low heat. When butter has melted, add onion and jalapeño peppers, and sauté for 5 minutes. Add bacon and cook until crisp. Add fatback and brown well.

Add tomatoes, stir, and cook for 20 minutes over low heat.

Cook pasta until al dente. Drain quickly and pour into sauce. Toss, sprinkle with grated cheese, and pour into serving bowl. Serve immediately.

4 servings

Enna

Penne with Black Olive Sauce

PENNE ALLE OLIVE NERE

The first time I was served this dish, I was put off at first by the
black sauce. However, one taste convinced me that
here was a real winner.

2 tablespoons olive oil

3 tablespoons butter

1 stalk celery, diced

1 small onion, peeled and diced

½ red bell pepper, seeded and diced

¼ cup dry white wine

2 tablespoons black olive paste
(available in specialty food shops)

6 tablespoons heavy cream

2 ounces oil-cured black olives, pitted
and halved

1 pound penne or rigatoni

2 tablespoons grated Swiss cheese

Black pepper to taste

Heat olive oil and 2 tablespoons butter in a large skillet over moderate
heat. Add celery, onion, and red bell pepper, and sauté until vegetables are
soft. Add wine and cook for 2 minutes. Stir in olive paste, cream, and olives,
and remove from heat.

Cook pasta until al dente. Drain well and pour into the skillet with the
olive sauce. Add remaining butter, grated Swiss cheese, and grind on some
black pepper. Sauté for a minute or two to heat through. Transfer to a warmed
bowl and serve.

4 servings

Small Ribbon Pasta in Squid Sauce

TAGLIATELLE AI CALAMARI

If you are among the growing number of people who regard squid as a marvelous type of seafood, you will really enjoy this succulent dish.

2 tablespoons olive oil

1 large onion, peeled and very thinly sliced

½ pound squid, cut into rings (you may use fresh or frozen)

½ ounce ripe black olives, pitted and diced

1 28-ounce can of Italian peeled tomatoes, drained and chopped

6 large fresh basil leaves or 1 teaspoon dried basil

1 pound flat egg noodles or fettuccine

Basil leaves for garnish

Heat olive oil in a large skillet, add onion and sauté until golden brown. Stir in squid and cook for 10 minutes, or until squid has lightly browned. Add olives, tomatoes, and basil, and simmer for 10 minutes.

In the meantime, cook pasta until al dente. Drain pasta and toss into the skillet with the sauce, stirring gently. Cook for 2 minutes over low heat. Pour into a bowl, garnish with basil leaves, and serve.

4 servings

Taormina

The steep hills of Taormina are covered with orange and lemon groves.

Pappardelle with Lemon and Orange Sauce

The plentiful supply of citrus fruit in the south of Italy undoubtedly inspired this tantalizing, unusual recipe.

Zest of 1 large lemon, julienned

Zest of 1 medium orange, julienned

3 tablespoons butter

Juice of 1 large lemon, strained

1/2 cup heavy cream

1 pound pappardelle, unridged lasagne, or long, flat pasta

Salt to taste

1/4 cup chopped fresh parsley

1 tablespoon freshly ground black pepper

Fill a saucepan with water and bring to a boil. Add the lemon and orange zests and boil for 1 minute. Drain in a colander.

Melt the butter in a saucepan, then remove the pan from the heat. Add lemon juice and stir. Set aside.

In another saucepan, bring heavy cream to a boil and add zests. Lower heat to a simmer and cook for 5 minutes. Set aside.

Cook pasta until al dente. Drain well and toss with butter–lemon juice sauce.

Pour pasta into a sauté pan. Add zests, cream mixture, and a dash of salt. Cook over high heat for 1 minute. Pour into a serving bowl, sprinkle with chopped parsley and black pepper. Serve immediately.

4 servings

Egg Noodles, Fisherman's Style

TAGLIATELLE DEL PESCATORE

In the picturesque Sicilian town of Cefalù, I relished this happy combination of pasta and seafood.

6 tablespoons olive oil

1 medium onion, peeled and diced

1 medium carrot, peeled and minced

1 stalk celery, minced

4 canned Italian peeled plum tomatoes, drained and chopped

Salt and pepper to taste

2 medium zucchini, sliced into thin rounds

1-pound can mussels

1-pound can minced clams

½ cup chopped fresh parsley

½ cup dry white wine

1 pound long, flat egg noodles

In a saucepan, heat 2 tablespoons olive oil. Add onion, carrot, and celery, and sauté until onion is translucent. Add tomatoes and salt and pepper, and cook, uncovered, over moderate heat for 15 minutes. Set aside.

In a large skillet, heat 4 tablespoons olive oil over high heat. Add zucchini rounds and fry, turning once, until they are as crisp as potato chips. Drain zucchini chips on paper towels.

In a saucepan, cook mussels and clams in their liquid over moderate heat. Add chopped parsley and wine, cover, and cook for 5 minutes.

Cook pasta until al dente. Drain well. Toss with tomato sauce, add clams and mussels, toss, and heat for 3 minutes. Pour into a serving bowl. Toss with zucchini chips, top with some more chopped fresh parsley, and serve immediately.

4 servings

Penne with Fish Sauce

PENNE DEL MARE

The special flavors of capers and green olives are so evocative of southern Italy.

4 tablespoons olive oil

I medium onion, peeled and diced

2 cloves garlic, peeled and crushed

½ pound fresh anchovies, scaled and washed, heads and tails removed, and halved

I 28-ounce can Italian peeled plum tomatoes, chopped

I 6½-ounce can tuna packed in oil, drained and flaked

¼ cup white wine

Salt and pepper to taste

¼ cup chopped fresh parsley

I pound penne rigate or rigatoni

I tablespoon capers, rinsed

2 ounces stuffed green olives, rinsed and sliced

Preheat oven to 400°F.

Heat olive oil in a large skillet. Add onion and garlic, and sauté until onion is translucent. Add anchovies and cook for 2 minutes. Remove anchovies with slotted spoon and set aside. Add tomatoes and tuna to skillet, cook over moderate heat, stirring, for 5 minutes. Add wine and salt and pepper, and simmer for 15 minutes. Near the end of this cooking time, add parsley and anchovies.

Cook pasta until al dente. Drain well. Pour pasta into an ovenproof dish, toss with half the sauce, then cover with remaining sauce, capers, and olives. Bake for 5 minutes. Serve immediately.

4 servings

Sailors' Pasta

BUCATINI MARINARA

If you're a garlic lover, add an extra clove or
two to this sailors' delight.

4 tablespoons olive oil

½ large onion, peeled and diced

I clove garlic, peeled and crushed

½ stalk celery, diced

½ carrot, peeled and diced

I ounce dried mushrooms, rehydrated
for I hour, drained, and diced

I 6½-ounce can tuna packed in oil,
drained and flaked

I-pound can Italian peeled plum
tomatoes, drained and chopped

Salt and pepper

I-pound can mussels, drained (saving
½ cup liquid)

7 ounces canned baby shrimp, drained

I pound bucatini or perciatelli

5 fresh basil leaves, torn

In a large saucepan, heat olive oil over moderate heat. Add onion, garlic, celery, and carrot, and sauté until onion is translucent. Add mushrooms, and cook for 2 minutes. Add tuna, tomatoes, and salt to taste, and simmer for 20 minutes. Add mussels, shrimp, mussel liquid, bring to a boil, and cook for 5 minutes. Remove from heat.

Cook pasta until al dente. Drain well. Pour into sauce and toss. Transfer to a serving bowl, add pepper to taste, and garnish with fresh basil. Serve hot.

4 servings

Penne Pasta, Sicilian Style

PENNE ALLA SICILIANA

This popular pasta is traditionally served on Christmas Eve
as a late supper before Midnight Mass.

4 tablespoons olive oil

I medium onion, peeled and diced

2 cloves garlic, peeled and crushed

I-pound can Italian peeled plum
   tomatoes, drained and chopped

Salt and pepper

I pound fresh sardines, scaled, cleaned,
   boned, and cut into I-inch pieces

I small bulb of fresh fennel, diced

I ounce raisins, soaked in warm water
   for ½ hour and drained

I tablespoon pignoli (pine nuts)

I pound penne rigate or rigatoni

Heat olive oil in a large saucepan over moderate heat. Add onion and garlic and sauté until both are golden. Add tomatoes and salt and pepper to taste, and cook for 10 minutes. Add sardines, fennel, raisins, and pignoli, and cook for 10 minutes.

In the meantime, cook pasta until al dente. Drain well. Pour into a serving bowl, toss with sauce, and serve.

4 servings

Spaghetti, Grocer's Style

SPAGHETTI ALLA MODA DROGHIERE

Nutmeg, cinnamon, and cloves lend a strong
Middle Eastern flavor to this dish.

1 tablespoon butter

2 tablespoons olive oil

1 scallion, chopped

¼ pound ground veal

¼ pound Italian sausage, skinned, and
crumbled

1 sprig fresh rosemary or ¼ teaspoon
dried rosemary

½ cup dry red wine

1 cup crushed Italian plum tomatoes

Salt and pepper to taste

Dash nutmeg

1 whole clove

Dash cinnamon

1 pound spaghetti

¼ pound mozzarella cheese, cubed

1 tablespoon grated Parmesan cheese

In a large saucepan, melt butter and olive oil over moderate heat. Add scallion and sauté until golden. Add veal and sausage, adjust heat to high, and brown meat well, stirring with a wooden spoon. Lower heat and add rosemary and wine, and cook until the wine has evaporated. Stir in tomatoes and salt and pepper. Stir in nutmeg, clove, and cinnamon, and cook for 3 to 4 minutes. If sauce is too thick, add a few tablespoons of hot water. Remove from heat and set aside.

Cook pasta until al dente. Drain well. Remove clove and rosemary sprig from sauce. Add pasta and toss well.

Add mozzarella, toss, sprinkle with grated cheese. Pour into serving bowl and serve.

4 servings

From the Messina beach, the shores of Reggio Calabria are visible in the distance.

Zigzag Pasta with Bell Pepper Sauce
MALTAGLIATI AI PEPERONI

I first enjoyed this pasta dish on a warm afternoon at a harborside restaurant facing the Strait of Messina. To this day I can almost hear the gentle lapping of the water against the wharf. After much cajoling, the owner and chef, Don Peppino, gave me the recipe.

1 cup plus 2 tablespoons all-purpose flour

2 extra-large eggs

1 scant tablespoon tomato paste

¼ cup water

Salt and pepper to taste

4 bell peppers, 2 red and 2 yellow, roasted

4 walnuts, shelled

2 cloves garlic, peeled and minced

2 tablespoons grated Parmesan or Pecorino Romano cheese

3 tablespoons olive oil

2 tablespoons heavy cream

2 tablespoons minced parsley

To make pasta dough: Combine 1 cup flour, eggs, tomato paste, and a little water (about ¼ cup), a dash of salt, and prepare pasta according to instructions on page 4. Roll dough into a ball, flour it lightly, and divide into 2 pieces. Place dough on a floured surface and roll out each piece into a very thin rectangle. Dust the rectangles with flour and roll into cylinders. Using a sharp knife, cut the cylinders into zigzags so as to make many small triangles. Sprinkle the triangles with flour and lay them on a tray, making sure they don't overlap. Set aside.

To make Bell Pepper Sauce: Place roasted peppers, walnuts, garlic, grated cheese, olive oil, and cream into the bowl of a food processor fitted with the metal blade. Process for one minute.

Add salt, pepper, and parsley to the bell pepper sauce, pour into a saucepan, and heat until barely hot over a very low flame. Cook pasta until al dente, about 6 minutes. Lift from water, using a slotted spoon, and gently add to the sauce in the pan, stir lightly, and serve immediately.

4 servings

Corleone

Lionhearted Spaghetti

SPAGHETTI DEL CORLEONE

This dish is as hearty and earthy as the good people of the town for which it was named.

2 tablespoons olive oil

1 small onion, peeled and diced

1 jalapeño pepper, minced, or
   1 tablespoon hot pepper flakes

1-pound can Italian peeled plum
   tomatoes, drained and chopped

½ cup olive oil (for frying eggplant)

2 large eggplants, peeled and sliced
   into ¼-inch pieces, and processed
   as described on page 2

1 pound spaghetti

½ pound mozzarella cheese, cubed

¼ cup grated Pecorino Romano or
   Parmesan cheese

In a large saucepan, heat 2 tablespoons olive oil over moderate heat. Add onion and jalapeño pepper, and sauté until onion is golden brown. Add tomatoes, adjust heat to high, and cook for 10 minutes. Lower heat and simmer, covered, for 10 minutes.

In a nonstick skillet, heat ½ olive oil over moderate heat. When oil is very hot (almost smoking), fry the eggplant slices until golden brown on both sides. Remove with a slotted spoon and place on paper towels to drain.

Cook pasta until al dente. Drain well and toss with tomato sauce. Add mozzarella, grated cheese, and eggplant slices. Toss gently and serve very hot.

4 servings

The Aeolian Islands are seven little dots of land in the sea just off the northeast coast of Sicily.

Aeolian Islands Pasta

PENNE DELLE EÓLIE

Although the anchovies are optional, they give this dish
a certain piquant taste.

4 tablespoons olive oil

3 large cloves garlic, peeled and minced

4 small anchovies (optional), canned

I small eggplant, diced

I zucchini, diced

2 cups Basic Tomato Sauce (page 3)

8 oil-cured black olives or regular black olives, pitted and halved

I scant teaspoon capers, rinsed

I large yellow bell pepper, roasted, peeled and sliced into ribbons

5 fresh basil leaves, minced

Salt

I pound penne rigate or any short tubular pasta, such as rigatoni

¼ cup grated Pecorino Romano or Parmesan cheese

In a large saucepan, heat oil over low heat, add garlic, and sauté until golden. Add anchovies, if desired, eggplant, zucchini, and cook for 3 minutes. Stir in tomato sauce, increase heat to moderate, and bring sauce to a boil. Lower heat and simmer for 10 minutes.

Add olives, capers, roasted pepper, basil, and salt to taste. Cover and simmer on low heat for 15 minutes, stirring often.

Cook pasta until al dente, drain, and toss with sauce. Pour into a pasta bowl. Sprinkle with grated cheese and serve very hot.

4 servings

Nuoro

Pasta in a Dense Broccoli Sauce

PASTA E BROCCOLI CON BRODO DENSO

This dish is indeed deliciously dense because the pasta is cooked right in the sauce!

1½ quarts water

1 chicken bouillon cube, crushed

1 large head fresh broccoli, broken into florets

2 large cloves garlic, peeled and crushed

1 teaspoon hot pepper flakes

2 tablespoons olive oil

1 pound bucatini, perciatelli, or spaghetti

Salt and pepper to taste

2 tablespoons grated Pecorino Romano cheese

In a large saucepan, bring water to a boil. Add bouillon cube and broccoli, and cook for 20 minutes. Turn off heat.

In a skillet, sauté garlic and hot pepper in olive oil, for 5 minutes.

Over high heat, return broccoli to a boil, then add uncooked pasta, and cook until pasta is al dente. Stir in sautéed garlic, hot pepper, oil, and salt and pepper. Pour into a serving bowl and sprinkle with grated cheese. Serve.

4 servings

Ravioli with Garden Sauce

RAVIOLI DEL ORTO

The light taste of summer in this dish intensifies
if you use garden-fresh vegetables.

1 carrot, peeled and cut into 3 pieces

1 medium onion, peeled and quartered

½ cup chopped fresh parsley, plus
    extra for garnish

1 stalk celery

2 tablespoons butter

1 cup dry white wine

Salt and pepper to taste

5 ounces frozen peas, defrosted

1-pound can Italian peeled plum
    tomatoes, drained and chopped

1 pound frozen cheese ravioli

In a food processor fitted with the metal blade, process carrot, onion, parsley, and celery with two short pulses.

Melt butter in a skillet over moderate heat, add processed vegetables, and sauté for 5 minutes. Add wine and salt and pepper, and simmer for 20 minutes. Add peas and tomatoes, and continue to simmer for 20 minutes.

Cook ravioli according to package directions. Drain well, transfer to a serving bowl, and toss gently with sauce. Garnish with fresh parsley and serve.

4 servings

Egg Noodles with Rich Sauce

TAGLIATELLE ALLA RICCA

A crisp green salad is very refreshing after this deliciously rich dish.

4 tablespoons butter

2 tablespoons olive oil

½ medium onion, peeled and diced

½ stalk celery, diced

1 carrot, peeled and diced

¾ pound veal, diced

2¼ cups Basic Tomato Sauce (page 3), or use canned

Salt and pepper

5½ ounces frozen peas

¾ pound fresh mushrooms, wiped clean

1 pound flat egg noodles

2 cloves garlic, peeled and minced

2 tablespoons chopped fresh parsley

2¼ cups Bechamel Sauce (page 4)

½ cup grated Parmesan or Pecorino Romano cheese

In a skillet, melt butter and olive oil over moderate heat. Add onion, celery, and carrot and sauté until onion is translucent, not brown. Add the veal and sauté for 3 minutes. Add tomato sauce, salt and pepper to taste, cover, and simmer for 10 minutes. Add peas and continue to simmer for 20 minutes. Slice half the mushrooms into thin slices and dice the other half.

Mince the garlic and parsley together and sauté for 3 minutes in 1 tablespoon butter and 2 tablespoons olive oil, then add all the mushrooms, salt and pepper, and sauté on medium heat for 10 minutes. Meanwhile, cook noodles until al dente, drain quickly, and set aside.

Preheat broiler.

Toss noodles with the bechamel and tomato sauces and the mushrooms. Pour into a well-buttered ovenproof dish. Sprinkle with grated cheese and place under broiler until lightly browned. Serve immediately.

4 servings

Pasta with Meat Sauce

MACARONCINI AL RAGÙ

Sardegna is home to large flocks of sheep, which accounts
for the ground lamb in this intriguing sauce.

1 tablespoon butter

3 tablespoons olive oil

1 carrot, peeled and diced

1 stalk celery, diced

1 medium onion, peeled and sliced
thinly

¼ cup minced fresh parsley

½ ounce diced porcini mushrooms (or
any imported dried mushrooms),
rehydrated in lukewarm water for 1
hour and drained through a fine
mesh strainer

½ pound ground lean lamb

½ cup dry white wine

2 tablespoons tomato paste, diluted
with 1 tablespoon of water

Salt and pepper to taste

1 pound penne, mostaccioli, or any
short pasta

¼ cup grated Pecorino Romano or
Parmesan cheese

In a large saucepan, melt butter and olive oil over medium heat. Add
carrot, celery, onion, and parsley. Cook until onion is soft and translucent.
Add mushrooms and cook for 10 minutes.

Stir in ground lamb, and cook over low heat until browned. Add wine and
cook until evaporated. Add diluted tomato paste, and salt and pepper, and
cook, covered, on low heat for 40 minutes.

Cook pasta until al dente. Drain well, toss with sauce, mix, pour into
bowl, sprinkle with grated cheese, and serve.

4 servings

Tricolored Egg Noodles

TAGLIATELLE AI TRE COLORI

The noodles themselves are not tricolored; this dish absorbs its color from the ingredients in the sauce.

2 tablespoons olive oil

1 clove garlic, peeled and crushed

3 medium zucchini, julienned

2 bell peppers, 1 red, 1 yellow, seeded and julienned

2 tablespoons paprika

1/2 pint yogurt

2 tablespoons chopped fresh parsley

1/2 pint heavy cream

10 Greek black olives or regular black olives, pitted and halved

1 pound long, flat egg noodles

1 small envelope of saffron

1/4 cup grated sharp Pecorino Romano cheese

Heat oil in a large saucepan over moderate heat. Add garlic and cook until golden. Adjust heat to high, add zucchini and bell peppers, and sauté for 3 minutes. Lower heat to simmer and cook, uncovered, for 20 minutes. Add paprika, cover, and cook for 1 minute. Add yogurt, parsley, and cream, mix well and remove saucepan from heat. Add olives.

Cook noodles until al dente in salted water along with saffron. Drain noodles quickly, pour into serving bowl, toss with sauce, sprinkle with grated cheese, and serve.

4 servings

A sentimental favorite

Lovers' Pasta
PENNE DEGLI AMANTI

Le Vecchie Città d'Italia (The Old Cities of Italy)—Every old Italian city claims to be the city of love. When you visit Italy, you will have to make the decision—is only one of them that city, are several, or are they all? In any case, whatever your choice, you may be inspired to make the following dish, which is perfect for Valentine's Day. According to tradition, heart-shaped red and yellow bell peppers remind us of the love that resides within the human heart. This dish certainly offers a delicious way to say "I love you."

1 large yellow bell pepper, halved and seeded

1 large red bell pepper, halved and seeded

1 tablespoon butter

2 tablespoons olive oil

1 medium onion, peeled and diced

Salt and pepper to taste

¼ cup dry white wine

6 canned Italian plum tomatoes, drained and chopped

1 pound penne rigate or rigatoni

4 fresh basil leaves, chopped along with ¼ cup fresh parsley

3 heaping tablespoons grated Parmesan cheese

Bring a large pot of water to a boil. Add bell peppers and boil for 1 minute. Remove from water with a slotted spoon. Slip skins off peppers and cut them into large slices, then, with a heart-shaped cookie cutter, cut out as many hearts as you can.

Melt butter and olive oil in a large saucepan over moderate heat. Add onion and sauté until golden. Add pepper hearts and sauté over high heat for 2 minutes. Lower heat to moderate and season with salt and pepper. Add wine and simmer until wine evaporates. Add tomatoes, a pinch of salt, and simmer for 15 minutes.

Cook pasta until al dente. Drain well. Transfer to the pan with the sauce, stir, and add chopped basil and parsley. Pour into a serving bowl, sprinkle with grated cheese, toss again, and serve.

4 servings

Local Wines and Restaurants

Some restaurants where foods typical of the regions can be tasted and regional wines can be sampled:

Region	City	Restaurant
Molise	Campobasso	Da Emma Via Ziccardi, 94

A characteristic osteria in the tiny old city center, Da Emma sits proudly in a narrow, serpentine street. If you want to savor the best Molisano cuisine, Emma, her husband, Cecchino Cerone, and their daughter Christina know all the secrets of this distinctive regional fare.

The DOC Wines of Molise

Biferno (dry red, pink, and white)
Pentro (dry red, pink, and white)

Locally produced table wines are rather strong and quite forgettable.

Region	City	Restaurant
Puglia	Bari	La Pignata
		Corso Vittoria Emanuele, 173

La Pignata is a modern restaurant in the center of the city. Antonio Vincenti, in the kitchen, and his brother Franco, in the dining room, have made this the best restaurant in Bari. The menu is an absolute encyclopedia of Pugliese cuisine, and the dishes are precise expressions of Barese cooking.

The DOC Wines of Puglia

Puglia produces millions of barrels of wine that are sent all over Italy and France to be mixed with local wines for general consumption. However, here are some of the better bottled wines:

Aleatico di Puglia (sweet red)
Alezio (dry red and rosé)
Brindisi (dry red)
Castel del Monte (dry red)
Donna Marzia (dry white and red), not DOC but an exceptional wine
Rosso Barletta (dry red)

Region	City	Restaurant
Campania	Napoli	Il Drago Riviera di Chiaia, 270

Situated in the center of the "aristocratic" zone of Naples, Il Drago is lovingly supervised by the owner, Mario, and his wife, who personally prepare the traditional Neapolitan home-style dishes. You can choose your own live fresh fish from the seawater tank in the entrance.

The DOC Wines of Campania

Fiano d'Avellino (red)

Greco di Tufo (dry white)

Solopaca (dry red)

Taurasi (dry red)

The table wines of the region are good to passable.

Region	City	Restaurant
Basilicata	Matera	Al Bocconcino Vico Lombardo, 52

Al Bocconcino is a small two-room restaurant. One room opens to the stupendous view of the Barisani Mountains. Traditional local dishes are cooked by the proprietor with an imaginative personal touch, and are served with quiet professionalism by his son.

The DOC Wine of Basilicata

Only one qualifies:

Aglianico del Vulture (dry red)

Other good wines include:

Aglianico dei Colli Lucani (dry red)
Asprino (white sparkling)
Malvasia della Lucania (white dry and sweet)
Montepulciano di Basilicata (dry red)
Moscato del Vulture (sweet white dessert wine)

Table wines are unremarkable.

Region	City	Restaurant
Calabria	Catanzaro	La Griglia Via Poerio, 26

Located right in the center of town, La Griglia has room for only fifty customers. If you can get in, you are expected to walk into the kitchen and ask Mamma Adelaide for her suggestions for dinner. Waiting to serve you in the dining room is papa, Mimmo Pompea, and their son. It's hard to find a restaurant more Calabrian than this one.

The DOC Wines of Calabria

Cirò (red and white)

Donnici (dry red)

Greco di Bianco (sweet white)

Lamezia (dry red)

Melissa (dry white)

Pollino (dry red)

Sant' Anna di Isola Capo Rizzuto (dry red and white)

Savuto (dry red and pink)

Table wines include:

Lacrima di Castrovillari (dry and sweet red)

Moscato (dessert wine)

Region	City	Restaurant
Sicilia	Palermo	Charleston
		Piazzale Ungheria, 30

The Charleston has been the most famous restaurant in Sicily for sixty years. Offering the finest Sicilian fare in the heart of modern Palermo, the Charleston is considered a point of reference in the history of Sicilian cuisine.

The DOC Wines of Sicily

Alcamo (dry white)

Cerasuolo di Vittoria (dry red)

Etna (dry red, pink, and white)

Faro (dry red)

Malvasia delle Lipari (excellent dessert wine)

Marsala (dry, semidry, and sweet)

Moscato di Pantelleria (sweet white)

Passito di Pantelleria Tanit (very sweet, made from raisins)

Table wines include:

Corvo

Faustus

Regaleali

Region	City	Restaurant
Sardegna	Alghero	La Lepanto Via Carlo Alberto, 135

La Lepanto is a combination hotel-restaurant. The chef, Moreno Cecchini, has become the foremost interpreter of traditional Sardinian fare. His specialty is the cuisine of Alghero, which is actually Catalán (Spanish) in origin. The menu and food are splendid.

The DOC Wines of Sardegna

Campidano di Terralba (dry red)

Cannonau di Sardegna (red and pink, dry or sweet)

Carignano del Sulcis (red and pink)

Malvasia di Cagliari (dessert wine)

Nuragus di Cagliari (dry white, the best-known and most drunk Sardinian wine)

Vernaccia di Oristano (the most celebrated wine of Sardegna; compares favorably with the best Spanish sherries)

At best, the table wines are not bad; at worst, they can be used as vinegar.

Chapter 4

Meals and Memories of Calabria, Reminiscences and Recipes

My roots are in Reggio Calabria, where my parents were raised and married, and the following reminiscences and recipes only scratch the surface of my experiences there. The tastes and flavors of certain foods are powerful stimulants to beautiful memories. Indeed, the people and meals described in this chapter bring back many pleasant hours spent in the places and with the people significantly linked to my mother and father. With this in mind, I am sure that you will savor not only the excellence of the recipes, but also the tenderness of the human bonds and relationships they represent.

Marietta La Bozzetta

Marietta La Bozzetta is the eighty-year-old godchild of my dear deceased mother. For me, each visit to Italy gives me the opportunity to spend time with Marietta and her children: Franco, Sandro, Mimy, and Ginny. The hospitality of this family to me is often overwhelming. Although we are not related by blood or marriage, they treat me as one of their own.

Marietta often recounts how, during the terrible years of World War II, Reggio Calabria suffered bombings from the Allied forces. Many times her family was without food, water, and other necessities; the only thing that kept them alive was the huge packages of food and clothing that my mother sent once a month to her extended family in Italy.

In 1965, one year after my ordination to the priesthood, my brother Oreste and I brought our mother with us to Italy. She had not returned to Reggio Calabria for forty-five years. We spent ten unforgettable days with the La Bozzetta family.

I love this wonderful lady because she is my surrogate mother in Italy, and her whole family is filled with accomplished cooks. The following recipes come from their bountiful kitchens. I know you will enjoy them as much as I do. Since Marietta was the teacher of her family's culinary art, I begin this section with one of her own favorites.

Marietta's Home-Style Pasta

PASTA INCASATA ALLA MARIETTA

This is a very rich pasta dish that is made only for special
occasions. It's filling, but oh so good!

½ cup vegetable oil (for frying
    eggplant)

1 large eggplant, peeled and thinly
    sliced, and processed as described
    on page 2

¼ cup olive oil

1 large onion, peeled and diced

2 cloves garlic, peeled and minced
    or crushed

1 pound lean pork, diced

1 cup dry white wine

2 cups Basic Tomato Sauce (page 3),
    or use canned

1 tablespoon sugar

¼ pound Genoa or hard Italian salami,
    julienned

4 hard-boiled eggs, shelled and sliced

¼ pound provolone cheese, diced

1 pound rigatoni, ziti, penne, or any
    short pasta

¼ cup grated Parmesan cheese

Heat vegetable oil in a sauté pan over medium heat. Add eggplant and
fry until browned on both sides. Remove from pan with a slotted spoon and
set aside on paper towels to drain.

In a large saucepan, heat olive oil over medium heat. Add onion, garlic,
and pork, and cook until pork is well browned. Add wine and cook for 5
minutes, then stir in tomato sauce and sugar. Cover, lower heat, and simmer
for 30 minutes. Stir in eggplant, salami, eggs, and provolone, and simmer for
10 minutes more.

Cook pasta until al dente. Drain well and pour into a serving bowl. Toss
with most of the sauce, and sprinkle with grated cheese. Reserve a little sauce
to add to individual servings. Serve immediately.

6 servings

Clelia Vita La Bozzetta

These pasta dishes are magnificently prepared and joyfully served in the home of Sandro La Bozzetta, Marietta's second oldest son, who is a successful civil engineer in Reggio Calabria. Clelia Vita, his lovely wife, hails from Locri, an ancient town founded by Greek colonizers about 2,500 years ago. In fact, present-day Locri is very near the site of the ancient city of the legendary Sybarites, known for their exquisite and luxurious cuisine.

Surely Clelia has Sybaritic blood in her veins because the aromas wafting from her kitchen make one's taste buds tingle. She is a delightful woman who is devoted to her profession as a caseworker for the government social services system, and to her husband and three children: Cinzia, a Doctor of Jurisprudence; Claudia, a university student of Jurisprudence; and Melania, a university student of modern languages. The two eldest daughters are engaged to be married. Cinzia has been engaged to Pino Chirico for nine years, but they will not marry untll Pino is able to find secure employment as a professional land surveyor in Reggio Calabria. When they wed, they'll move into an apartment that her father bought for her ten years ago. (It is not unusual in Calabria for couples to be engaged for ten to twelve years before they finally marry and raise a family.)

When I am in Clelia's presence, her culinary expertise, combined with her incomparable sense of humor, make me eat like a horse and laugh until I hurt. To know Clelia is to love her. She is completely devoted to her family and her work. In fact, her mother-in-law, Marietta, tells me often how Clelia is not a daughter-in-law but a true daughter. I am sure you will use these fantastic recipes again and again.

Clelia's Lasagne

LASAGNE ALLA CLELIA

This is not your ordinary lasagne because it is not baked,
which makes it a perfect in-a-hurry meal.

3 tablespoons butter

5 ounces mortadella (Italian baloney)
   or boiled ham, sliced into thin
   matchsticks

1 pound lasagne, mafalde, or fettuccine

4 large egg yolks

6 tablespoons grated Pecorino Romano
   or Parmesan cheese

Salt and pepper

Melt butter in sauté pan over low heat. Add mortadella or ham, increase heat to medium, and cook for 5 minutes.

Cook pasta until al dente, drain quickly, pour into serving dish. Toss with cooked mortadella or ham.

In a bowl, beat egg yolks with 3 tablespoons grated cheese and salt and pepper to taste. Toss with the lasagne. Season with more black pepper and 3 tablespoons grated cheese. Serve very hot.

4 servings

Clelia's Spaghetti

SPAGHETTI ALLA CLELIA

Though Clelia puts no garlic or onion in this dish, the sauce is so refreshing that they won't be missed.

⅔ cup olive oil

1-pound can Italian peeled plum tomatoes, drained and chopped

10 fresh basil leaves, torn

5 ounces mortadella or boiled ham, julienned

Salt and pepper

1 pound spaghetti

In a large saucepan, heat oil over low heat. Add tomatoes, basil, mortadella or ham, and salt and pepper to taste. Cook sauce, covered, for 30 minutes.

Cook pasta until al dente. Drain well and add to sauce. Toss well and cook, uncovered, for 5 more minutes. Pour into a serving dish and serve immediately.

4 servings

Penne Pasta with
Red Bell Pepper Sauce

PENNE AI PEPERONI DI CLELIA

The natural sweetness of the red bell peppers is a delicious counterbalance to the tart spiciness of the eggplant.

1 tablespoon butter	½ pound mushrooms, sliced
3 tablespoons olive oil	1 small eggplant, diced
1 medium onion, peeled and diced	1 pound penne rigate or rigatoni
1 medium carrot, peeled and diced	1 cup heavy cream
2 small red bell peppers, seeded and diced	¼ cup grated Parmesan cheese

In a large saucepan, melt butter and olive oil over medium heat. Add onion and carrot, and sauté until onion is golden. Add bell peppers, mushrooms, and eggplant, stir and cook, uncovered, for ½ hour.

Cook pasta until al dente. Drain well and pour into a pasta bowl. Stir in cream and grated cheese. Add sauce, toss, and serve immediately.

4 servings

Gnocchi with Nettle Sauce

GNOCCHI ALLA ORTICHE DI CLELIA

Clelia made this smooth, tasty dish for me during one delightful visit.
Don't be put off by the nettle leaves; if you can't find them,
you can substitute spinach.

3 tablespoons butter

2 ounces fresh nettle leaves, boiled 3 minutes, drained, squeezed dry, and minced

½ cup heavy cream

½ cup milk

¼ cup grated Parmesan cheese

Salt and pepper

2¼ pounds frozen potato gnocchi

In a large skillet, melt butter over moderate heat. Add nettles and sauté for 2 minutes. Add cream, and lower heat to a simmer, and cook for 5 minutes. Add milk, grated cheese, a dash of salt, and pepper to taste.

Cook gnocchi until al dente, according to package directions. Drain well and pour into sauce and stir gently. Serve hot and pass extra Parmesan cheese.

4 servings

Penne with Four-Cheese Sauce

PASTA AI QUATTRO FORMAGGI DI CLELIA

A meal designed for cheese lovers—but, alas,
not for diet watchers.

1 tablespoon butter	2 ounces Bel Paese cheese, cubed
4 tablespoons flour	3 ounces Swiss cheese, cubed
½ quart milk	Salt and pepper
½ pound mozzarella cheese, cubed	1 pound penne rigate
2 ounces fontina cheese, cubed	¼ cup grated Parmesan cheese

In a large saucepan, heat butter over moderate heat. Add flour and stir until butter is absorbed, about 2 minutes. Do not brown.

Add milk, adjust heat to a simmer, add cheeses and cook, uncovered, for 10 minutes, stirring often. Season with salt and pepper to taste.

Cook pasta until al dente, drain well, pour into sauce, and heat for 2 minutes more. Toss and transfer to a pasta bowl. Serve immediately. Pass grated cheese.

4 servings

Macaroni with Meat Sauce, Locri Style

MACCARUNI CU RAGÙ

A mouthwatering meat sauce made with Italian sausage (be sure the sausage contains fennel seeds; they enhance the flavor).

5 tablespoons olive oil

5 links Italian sausage, skinned and crumbled

1 large pork chop, boned and cubed

½ large onion, peeled and diced

1 2-pound can Italian peeled plum tomatoes with liquid, chopped

Salt and pepper

1 pound bucatini or perciatelli

6 fresh basil leaves, torn

¼ cup grated dry ricotta or very sharp Pecorino Romano cheese

In a large saucepan, heat oil over moderate heat. Add sausage and pork, and cook until meat is well browned. Add onion and sauté until soft and translucent.

Add tomatoes and their liquid and salt and pepper to taste. Stir and simmer for 1 hour.

Cook pasta until al dente. Drain well and pour into a pasta bowl. Toss with sauce and meat. Sprinkle with basil and cheese. Serve immediately.

4 servings

Fusilli with Zucchini

FUSILLI ALLE ZUCCHINE DI CLELIA

It is best to make this dish when the zucchini crop is plentiful; pick
the smallest ones you can find because they have the most
flavor and almost no seeds.

1 tablespoon butter

3 tablespoons olive oil

2 cloves garlic, peeled and crushed

1 pound zucchini, cut into rounds

1 pound fusilli or any corkscrew pasta

2 tablespoons grated Parmesan cheese

1 tablespoon grated Pecorino Romano
cheese

¼ cup chopped fresh parsley

In a large skillet, melt butter and oil over moderate heat. Add garlic and
sauté until golden. Add zucchini and sauté for about 10 minutes.

Cook pasta until al dente. Drain well. Transfer to a serving dish and toss
with cooked zucchini. Sprinkle with grated cheeses and chopped parsley.
Serve.

4 servings

Chirico's Spaghetti with Tuna Sauce

SPAGHETTI CON TONNO CHIRICO

This recipe comes from Caterina Chirico, Cinzia La Bozzetta's future mother-in-law.

2 tablespoons olive oil

1 large clove garlic, peeled and crushed

1-pound can Italian peeled plum tomatoes, drained and chopped

1 6½-ounce can tuna packed in oil, drained and flaked

1 cup black olives, pitted and halved

1 pound spaghetti

In a large skillet, heat oil over medium heat. Add garlic and sauté until golden. Add tomatoes, and cook, uncovered, for 5 minutes. Add tuna and olives, and simmer, covered, for 20 minutes.

Cook pasta until al dente. Drain well and pour into skillet with sauce. Toss well and cook for another 5 minutes. Pour into a pasta bowl, and serve immediately.

4 servings

Domenica (Mimy) La Bozzetta Giovanella

Mimy is the oldest La Bozzetta daughter, and as stunning as Gina Lollobrigida in her youth. She is a teacher of the severely handicapped, who simply adore her. Her husband, Aurelio, is an important attorney in the region and an accomplished pilot. Her son Giuseppe is a professional musician, and Elena, her lovely daughter, is a student of modern languages at the University of Rome.

Her brothers, especially Sandro, constantly kid her about her inability in the kitchen. "She can't even make a good cup of coffee," Sandro repeats to all who will listen. But I can tell you that she is an exquisite cook. And when you sample the following recipes, I'm sure you will agree with me.

Shell Pasta in Pink Sauce

CONCHIGLIONI IN SALSA ROSA

An outrageously rich meal—but perhaps an occasional lapse
will not disqualify you from your diet program.

4 egg yolks

2 ounces heavy cream

2 ounces unsalted butter

¼ cup grated Parmesan cheese

Dash black pepper

Dash nutmeg

1 pound medium shell pasta

3 tablespoons grated Pecorino Romano
cheese

Preheat broiler.

In a food processor fitted with the plastic blade, combine egg yolks, cream, butter, grated cheese, pepper, and nutmeg, and process for 2 minutes.

Cook pasta until al dente, drain quickly, and pour into ovenproof dish. Mix sauce with cooked pasta. Sprinkle on the Pecorino Romano grated cheese. Place dish under the broiler just long enough to lightly brown the cheese, about 5 minutes. Serve immediately.

4 servings

On Monday, November 2, 1992, I arose early because it was All Souls' Day on the Catholic liturgical calendar. This is a special day for all Catholics, the day when the Church allows priests to celebrate three Masses in a row in memory of deceased friends and family. I intended to say Masses for my father, Giuseppe, my mother, Carmela, and my nephew Dominick.

I used my key to gain access to the recreation room right next to the chapel. As I walked down the dark hallway, I saw the eerie dancing of candlelight. Suddenly I stopped in complete shock—almost terror. There before me was the dead body of one of the aged, retired priests with whom I had talked two nights before. Don Francesco Canale's body was lying in state in a simple open coffin surrounded by six huge candles, with the flames reflected in his open eyes. I quickly murmured a prayer for his departed soul and went into the chapel to say my Masses.

That afternoon, after I ate a delicious plateful of baked rigatoni, Mimy served espresso and then went to her pantry and brought out dessert—a huge plateful of Ossi dei Morti, "Bones of the Dead" cookies designed to look like dried bleached bones. These cookies are always served on All Souls' Day in southern Italy. They are very sweet and are supposed to remind you to enjoy the sweetness of life, and also to remember that death is inevitable.

Baked Rigatoni

RIGATONI AL FORNO

This is a good make-ahead dish; prepare it, then keep refrigerated
until it's time to place it in the oven.

1 pound frozen spinach	½ cup milk
6 tablespoons butter	1 pound rigatoni
Dash salt and black pepper	½ cup Basic Tomato Sauce (page 3)
Dash nutmeg (optional)	3 tablespoons grated Parmesan cheese
1 cup ricotta cheese	

Cook the spinach according to the directions on the package. Drain and
squeeze as dry as you can.

In a sauté pan, melt 3 tablespoons butter over medium heat. Add spinach
and sauté for 1 minute. Season with a dash of salt and nutmeg, if desired,
and set aside.

In a bowl, vigorously mix ricotta with milk. Set aside.

Cook pasta until al dente and drain completely in a colander. Return to
pot and mix with 3 tablespoons butter.

Preheat oven to 350°F.

Butter an ovenproof dish and toss in one third of the rigatoni. Top with
the spinach. Add another layer of rigatoni and cover it with the ricotta cheese–
milk mixture. Top with the last of the rigatoni and cover with tomato sauce
and grated Parmesan cheese. Bake for 20 minutes. Let sit for 5 minutes before
serving.

4 servings

Spaghetti, Guitar Style

I've enjoyed this dish with fresh homemade pasta. The name refers to the fact that the sheets of pasta dough are pressed through a fine wire implement that resembles a large guitar.

2 tablespoons butter

2 tablespoons olive oil

1 large zucchini, sliced into thin rounds

3½ ounces pancetta, prosciutto, or boiled ham, minced

2 cloves garlic, peeled and minced or crushed in a garlic press

2 tablespoons fresh minced parsley

2 tablespoons fresh basil (if not available, add 2 more tablespoons parsley)

1 large onion, peeled and diced

1 tablespoon Scotch whiskey (optional)

1 pound spaghetti

Parsley and grated Parmesan cheese

In a large skillet, melt butter and oil over medium heat. Add zucchini and sauté until light brown on both sides. Remove zucchini from pan, place in large bowl, and set aside.

Add pancetta, garlic, aromatic herbs, and onion to the skillet and sauté until onion is lightly browned. Return zucchini to the pan. Add 1 tablespoon Scotch whiskey, if desired, and turn off heat.

Cook pasta until al dente and drain quickly. Add pasta to sauce, stir, and pour into a serving bowl. Sprinkle with a little chopped parsley and as much grated Parmesan cheese as you wish. Serve immediately.

4 servings

Maria (Geni) La Bozzetta Stilo

Geni is the youngest of the La Bozzetta children, a teacher by profession, and the acknowledged pastry chef of the family. Her desserts are the best I have ever tasted, but when her husband, Rocco, also a teacher, her children, Francesca, Maria Luisa, and little Domenico, and I are at her table for dinner, I cannot honestly say who is the best cook in the family. Perhaps it is Marietta, the matriarch, because they all learned their skills from her.

I must tell you about little Domenico. He is now a fourth grader, a straight-A student, and a charming little rascal. But when he was younger, I dubbed him "Il Terramoto" (The Earthquake), because he had so much energy that he was in constant motion. One day, when I was at dinner with Geni and her family, little Domenico stood up on his chair and literally threw himself on the table, which was already groaning under the weight of a seven-course meal. The table broke, and there was an explosion of food, drink, dishes, glasses, and silverware. He simply wanted attention and he certainly got it, lots of it. The "earthquake" was sent to his room screaming, and after everything was salvaged, the meal resumed. I was absolutely speechless as the whole family roared with laughter. I looked at Geni, who said, "Not to worry, he does that all the time."

Here are Geni's wonderful pasta recipes for you to enjoy—without the "earthquake," of course.

Geni's Special Macaroni

PENNE ALLA GENI

Geni, who teaches in a small mountain village, learned this zesty recipe from the mother of one of her students.

½ cup olive or vegetable oil (for frying eggplant)

2 small eggplants, cubed

1 tablespoon butter

4 tablespoons olive oil

½ onion, peeled and chopped

½ carrot, peeled and minced

½ stalk celery, finely diced

1 large red bell pepper, seeded and julienned

1 8-ounce can sliced mushrooms, drained

3 canned Italian plum tomatoes, diced

1 cup chicken or beef stock, or bouillon

½ cup heavy cream

2 slices boiled ham, julienned

Pepper to taste

1 pound penne rigate

¼ cup grated Parmesan cheese

In a large skillet, heat oil over moderate heat. Add eggplant and sauté until golden. Remove the eggplant with a slotted spoon and drain on paper towels. Wipe out the skillet. In the same skillet, melt butter and olive oil, over moderate heat. Add onion, carrot, and celery, and sauté until onion is translucent. Add bell peppers and sauté until soft, or about 10 minutes. Add mushrooms and wine, and cook until wine evaporates. Add tomatoes and cook for 5 minutes. Add stock and cook on low heat for 15 minutes. Stir in cream, eggplant, and ham. Season with pepper to taste.

Cook pasta until al dente. Drain well. Pour into sauce, stir, add grated cheese (if sauce is dry, add more cream). Pour into a pasta dish and serve.

6 servings

Mountain-Style Penne

Geni got this recipe from the mother of one of her students who lives in a remote mountain village, thus the name.

4 tablespoons olive oil

1 large onion, peeled and diced

1 clove garlic, peeled and crushed

1-pound can Italian peeled plum tomatoes, chopped

1 pound penne rigate

½ teaspoon dried oregano

½ cup heavy cream

¼ cup grated Parmesan cheese

In a large saucepan, heat oil over medium heat, add onion and garlic, and sauté until golden. Add tomatoes and cook, covered, for 20 minutes.

Cook pasta until al dente. Drain well. Pour into a pasta bowl and toss with sauce. Add oregano, cream, and grated cheese. Toss again and serve.

4 servings

Baked Egg Noodles

This is a rich Italian version of baked macaroni and cheese that bears no resemblance to the commercial products.

½ large onion, peeled and diced

4 tablespoons oil

2 cups Basic Tomato Sauce (page 3), or use canned

3 fresh basil leaves, minced

Salt

1 pound flat egg noodles

½ cup heavy cream

2 tablespoons butter

¼ cup grated Parmesan cheese

½ pound mozzarella cheese, cubed

½ pound provolone cheese, cubed

7 ounces boiled ham, diced

Preheat oven to 350°F.

In a skillet, sauté onion in olive oil until lightly browned. Add tomato sauce, basil, and salt to taste. Cover and cook over moderate heat for 20 minutes.

Cook noodles until al dente. Drain well. Pour into a pasta bowl, toss with half of the sauce. Add cream and toss.

In an ovenproof dish, place a layer of sauce, then a layer of pasta. Cover sparingly with sauce, add butter, half of the grated cheese, mozzarella, provolone, and ham. Cover with remaining pasta, sauce, and grated cheese. Bake for 20 minutes. Remove from oven and let stand for 5 minutes before serving.

4 servings

The Peasant Woman's Spaghetti

SPAGHETTI ALLA CAMPAGNOLA DI GENI

Here's a recipe from a peasant woman who was grateful to Geni
for being a wonderful teacher to her six children.

4 tablespoons olive oil

I large clove garlic, peeled and crushed

2-pound can Italian plum tomatoes
with liquid, coarsely chopped

3½ ounces pitted black olives, halved

4 tablespoons capers, rinsed

¼ cup fresh chopped parsley

I pound spaghetti

¼ cup grated sharp Pecorino Romano
or Parmesan cheese

¼ cup chopped fresh parsley

Salt and pepper to taste

In a saucepan, heat olive oil and sauté garlic until golden. Add tomatoes, olives, capers, and ½ of parsley, and cook for 30 minutes.

Cook pasta until al dente. Drain well. Add to the sauce in the pan and toss lightly. Toss with grated cheese, sprinkle with the rest of the parsley, and serve immediately in a pasta bowl.

4 servings

The Story of Natuzza Evolo

I must share the following experience with you. In 1992, the day before I left for my autumn trip to Italy, I received a magazine from Italy that is sent free of charge to anyone of Calabrian descent living abroad. In it was an article about a peasant woman, Natuzza Evolo, unable to read or write, who has lived in Paravati, a little mountain village in Calabria, all of her life. She is married and the mother of seven children.

The article reported that Natuzza was gifted with the stigmata, the outward wounds of Christ. For the past forty years, every Holy Week (the week before Easter) the wounds open and she sweats blood and suffers the Passion of Christ as described in the New Testament. The article reported that she is visited by hundreds of people every day. It also stated that she correctly and scientifically diagnoses illnesses; she bilocates (appears in the flesh to people all over Europe and at the same time never leaves her village), and the beloved deceased of her supplicants talk through her, giving them personal messages of hope and comfort. I decided then and there that I must visit this woman. Now, I am by nature and education skeptical of these kinds of occurrences, but out of curiosity, I wanted to see her face to face.

Sandro's daughter, Claudia, her fiancé, Sandro Turano, and I decided to visit Natuzza on Wednesday, November 4. We traveled by car, arriving at the village of Pavarati at 4:15 P.M. We asked an elderly gentleman where we could find Natuzza. He informed us that her doctors had forbidden her to receive visitors because she suffers from serious heart disease; however, if we went to the village church, she would be there for five o'clock Mass.

Of course, we went to the church immediately. It was 4:30, there were only a handful of people in church, and we took seats in the third pew before the altar. At 4:35, the church was suddenly bursting with people, and Natuzza, whom I recognized from her photograph in the magazine, walked in and knelt at the pew directly in front of me. She prayed for a few minutes, then she turned to me, arose from her kneeler, and kissed my hand while smiling. I was dressed in street clothes, but she gave me the customary Calabrian sign of respect for a priest.

The Mass began and Natuzza turned back to face the altar. At the sign of peace (a handshake before Holy Communion to demonstrate the solidarity of our faith), she turned, smiled, and took my hand in hers. After Mass was over, she was besieged by needy supplicants. I shall never forget that Mass celebrated in a village church in the mountains of Calabria, and of course I shall never forget Natuzza. I was convinced that I must tell this story in my book, because when I asked the parish priest where she would go after church, he responded simply: "Why, to her house, of course, to prepare pasta for her family."

That evening, after we returned from visiting with Natuzza, Claudia La Bozzetta's fiancé, Sandro Turano, gave me the following recipe. It is one of his favorite dishes.

Fusilli Macaroni with Roasted Red Peppers

PASTA ALLA LEONILDE

Leonilde is Sandro Turano's favorite aunt. She invented this recipe because she is allergic to tomatoes.

3 tablespoons olive oil

3 large red bell peppers, roasted, peeled, and sliced into long ribbons

Salt and pepper to taste

¼ cup chopped fresh parsley

1 pound fusilli or spaghetti

½ pint heavy cream

¼ cup grated Parmesan cheese

In a deep sauté pan, heat oil over medium heat. Lower heat to a simmer and add bell pepper. Add salt and pepper to taste. Cook for 3 minutes. Remove from heat.

Place bell peppers and oil in the bowl of a food processor fitted with the metal blade, and process for 1 minute. Return the sauce to the pan. Add parsley and cook for 3 minutes. Remove from heat.

Cook pasta until al dente. Drain well. Toss with heavy cream. Pour into pan with pepper sauce. Toss to coat pasta evenly. Pour into a serving bowl. Sprinkle with grated cheese and serve immediately.

4 servings

In Bova, I met Angelo Maisano. A stonemason by trade, he is an elegant gentleman in his seventies, one of Calabria's Grecanici, the descendants of the original Greek colonizers of the Ionian coast of Calabria. Their language, with a few modifications, is the classical Greek of 2,500 years ago.

Angelo attended school for only five years. Then, because of his large family's needs, he was apprenticed to a master stonemason; fifteen years later, he became a master stonemason.

He has received honors—comparable to the Nobel Prize in literature—from both the Italian and Greek governments as the primary poet laureate in the Grecanico language. This simple man with his limited schooling is a genius. Before leaving Bova, Angelo insisted that we travel to his *terreno* (a piece of land of an acre or more where he cultivates olives, almonds, fruits, vegetables, and herbs, and keeps a flock of sheep and goats that supply wool, meat, and milk, which is then processed into cheese). Outside a ramshackle shed, he insisted that I try his *caffè della campagna*, "countryside coffee," wine produced from his own grapes. That was the most powerful cup of coffee I had ever tasted. It was indeed a soporific, for I slept for the whole hourlong ride back to Reggio. The following recipe is from Angelo's kitchen:

Addictive Pasta, Bova Style

MAFALDE GOLOSE BOVESE

Once you try this dish you'll have no trouble figuring out the origin of its name. This is one addiction you won't mind cultivating.

4 tablespoons olive oil

½ large onion, peeled and diced

½ stalk celery, diced

½ carrot, peeled and diced

½ pound ground lamb

¼ pound Italian sausage, skinned and crumbled

I slice boiled ham, diced

I slice Canadian bacon, diced

½ ounce dried porcini mushrooms, soaked in I cup lukewarm water for I hour, drained through a fine mesh strainer (save liquid), and diced

½ cup dry white wine

2 cups Basic Tomato Sauce (page 3), or use canned

I tablespoon tomato paste

I tablespoon water

Salt and pepper

I pound mafalde or any long, thin, ridged macaroni

¼ cup grated Pecorino Romano Cheese

In a large saucepan, heat olive oil over medium heat. Add onion, celery, and carrot, and cook until onion is soft and translucent. Add ground lamb, sausage, ham, and Canadian bacon, and mushrooms. Cook over low heat, stirring, until meat is light brown.

Add wine, adjust heat to medium, and cook until wine evaporates. Add tomato sauce, tomato paste, water, and stir. Add mushroom liquid, and season with salt and pepper to taste. Simmer, covered, for 1 hour, stirring often.

Cook pasta until al dente and drain well. Pour into a pasta bowl, toss with lamb sauce, and serve immediately. Pass the grated cheese.

4 servings

Personal Reflections

On May 16, 1994, I celebrated my thirtieth year as a Roman Catholic priest. I was forced to retire from the ordinary active ministry because of illness.

I am now primarily an author of cookbooks. My cookbooks allow me to philosophize, theologize, and share my personal experiences. But my cookbooks do not pose a threat to anyone's belief or nonbelief. The recipes, historical commentaries, anecdotes, and opinions I relate are filtered through a view of the world that I drank in, along with the milk from my mother's breast, as an infant.

My upbringing was in the Italian tradition, where families are noted for their conspicuous attitudes of loyalty and allegiance. Even in the modern Italian family there exists a strict "order of the family," which views the family unit as central to the life of each individual. It also is characterized by a complex structure of rules governing the roles and attitudes of each member. Included in this worldview are the traditional concepts of family honor, pragmatic attitudes toward sex and religion, and a deep regard for food as the host of life.

Traditionally, the home is the site and source of all that gives meaning to life. To an Italian, a well-kept home indicates a sound family. Furniture that is durable symbolizes family stability and family strength. Most important of all, plentiful food, carefully prepared, is a sign of family well-being.

When I was a child, it was made clear that food was the symbol of the love our family had for us. It was the product of the back-breaking labor of our father and brothers, and it was prepared for us with care and love by our mother. It was, in a very emotional sense, a connection among my father, mother, five brothers, and one sister. Meals were a communion of the family and food was sacred because it was the medium of the intimate communion.

Many Italians consider the saying of a short prayer before meals as unnecessary because food comes from God and keeps us together. Why bless it again? The worse thing that a family can do at a meal is to have an intrusive television set blasting interference with conversation at the table.

I believe these values are well worth retaining because they represent a positive and stabilizing influence to family bonding.

Whether or not you agree with me, I wish you warm friends, good food, and long life.

Index

Index

Index